CREATING HEAVEN ON EARTH

CREATING HEAVEN ON EARTH

A GUIDE TO PERSONAL ASCENSION

BARBARA M. HARDIE

Crystal Clear Publishing
Tolland, Massachusetts
email: barbara@angelconnections.com
www.angelconnections.com

Cover Artwork: Sue Muldoon Images, LLC;
www.suemuldoonimages.com
Editing, Cover and Interior Design: provided by Ja-lene Clark
and Jo Ann Deck of www.gatherinsight.com

ISBN: 978-0-9837533-0-8
First Printing July 2011

Disclaimer
Creating Heaven on Earth: A Guide to Personal Ascension may con-
tain information that opposes traditional beliefs and some facts.
This is not meant to offend anyone. It is provided from the author's
personal experiences and spiritual perspective. The author is not
a medical practitioner and in no way is providing medical advice
or diagnosis, and therefore, strongly encourages anyone struggling
with the symptoms of Ascension or especially thoughts of suicide
to first, foremost and ALWAYS seek professional help. The information provided is strictly for information purposes only and the
author is not responsible for any actions taken by the reader.

Printed in the United States of America

Dedication

I would like to dedicate *Creating Heaven on Earth* to my wonderful team of Heavenly Helpers:

Aaron and Crystal — My Guardian Angels,
Jonathan — My Master Guide,
Jesus/Sananda — My Ascension Master,
and
Archangel Michael — My Ascension Angel.

Also included in this dedication are the many other Light Beings who have so lovingly come forward on my behalf. The assistance from all of these spiritual guides is very much appreciated and they made a huge difference in my life. Without their constant encouragement and assistance throughout the years, this book would not have become a reality. If you have not already made a connection with your Spiritual Team, I strongly suggest that you think seriously about doing so. Life is so much better once we learn to trust their guidance and know that their job is to help us along our journey here on Earth.

CREATING HEAVEN ON EARTH
TABLE OF CONTENTS

ACKNOWLEDGMENTS

There are so many individuals who have helped me along my path, and if only there was enough time or space to thank them individually. However, I would like to express special thanks to Flo D'Aleo and her daughter Jodi. I met Flo at a psychic fair about twenty-two years ago. Flo was manning the registration desk and said she was sorry but all the readers were booked right up to closing. Very disappointed with this information, I turned and started to leave. Flo promptly followed me to the door and handed me a flyer. Her daughter, Jodi, was offering an eight week psychic development program.

I just wanted a reading. I didn't want to learn how to do my own reading. At that time I thought only "special" people had the gift to communicate with the other side. Now I know we all have the ability if we want to. Anyway, Flo was such a nice lady and I didn't want to hurt her feelings so I took the flyer. Not wanting to litter the parking lot, I put it on the front seat of my car. Long story short, something inside of me (my Soul) nagged me to make the call and sign up for the classes. It is the best thing that has happened to me. I would not be as spiritually advanced as I am today if it were not for these two fine ladies being in my life, so I thank them for sticking with and putting up with me during the growth years.

Additionally, I would like to thank my friends, Sandy Cangemi and Lori Loiselle for all the help and support they have offered me over the years. I would also like to thank all the ladies from the Monday Night Meditation/ Healing Group for their friendship and support.

My Angels connected me with the next lady I would like to thank and that is Jo Ann Deck of GatherInsight. com. In meditation I had asked my angels to connect me with someone who could help me with getting my book ready for printing. Jo Ann and I met and I immediately sensed her passion and dedication for her work and for books in general. She has done the editing and has been a tremendous help. Thank you so much, Jo Ann. Jo Ann introduced me to her business partner Ja-lene Clark who did the cover and interior design and formatting. I thank both ladies for their dedication and prompt delivery.

INTRODUCTION

The birth of *Creating Heaven on Earth — A Guide to Personal Ascension* came about as a result of my "Awakening" Process, which then led to the Ascension Process. Since many individuals on the planet are in the Awakening or Ascension phase, and many more will be opening up as a result of the 2012 energy shifts, my angelic guidance prompted me to put some of what I learned and experienced about creation, the Soul, the issue of suicide, and Ascension into a book so that this information may help others who are also on this journey.

The "Awakening" process of my beginning to walk on my spiritual path was not easy for me. The tug at my Soul strings happened while working in the corporate world. I loved my job, the company I worked for, and the people I worked with. I was good at what I did and the pay and benefits were excellent. However, my Soul had other plans and I wasn't paying attention to the signs. I did notice that I was very "cranky," irritable all the time. Of course, that was NOT my fault. It was the fault of everyone else around me and I could prove it!

One night after an extremely stressful day, I reached up to God and asked for help in finding Inner Peace. I really don't know what I expected; I put the word out and forgot about it. Little by little I was lead to spiritual topics, angels specifically, and eventually I was like a sponge. I couldn't get enough and read several books, mostly on Angels, went to classes and joined a weekly meditation group. I was hooked! Even now, over twenty years later, I am still anxious to learn and teach whatever I can on spiritual topics. I was unaware of the power of "Ask and You Shall Receive" before I made my request, but God answered my prayer! I now possess INNER PEACE. I feel calm within no matter how much chaos is going on around me. My "aha" moment came when I finally realized that I was the cause of my own problems — not all those innocent, wonderful people around me.

I worked with the Angel Kingdom for about three years. At first it was all about me. I just wanted to receive information for my own benefit, not to share with others. The saying about public speaking being a fear worse than death was my truth at that time. Then in 1995, the Angels gave me the name "Angel Connections" for my business and said it was time for me to share with others what they had shared with me. I promised them I would, then FEAR set in and I didn't keep my promise. The Spirit World is so much smarter than we THINK we are. Jesus came to me in meditation and asked if I would do Him a favor. Being an ex-Catholic, I naturally said yes. "They" knew if I gave Jesus a yes, I would not renege on that promise. I left the corporate world and went full time into giving Angel Lectures and then organizing mind/

body/spirit expos.

My first scheduled lecture on Angels had quite a few people pre-registered, then I got cold feet. My stomach was queasy. My legs were shaky. I felt like I was going to collapse. I wanted to turn around and go home, but instead I called upon Jesus, who had gotten me into this in the first place (I was still at the point of blaming others), and asked Him to please help me calm down. At the point when I started to speak, instead of saying what I originally intended to say, I started to explain to the attendees that it was my first time public speaking and to please be patient with me. With that comment, I felt a calm, peaceful energy envelop the room and It stayed for the balance of the evening. When I think of how I struggled with life before I opened up, I don't know how I managed. Life is so much better and easier now. I would encourage EVERYONE to connect with their spiritual guidance to improve all areas of life.

While in the beginning phase of opening up to my spiritual guidance, I was like a yo-yo. When Spirit was with me in meditation, it seemed so real, but then my logical/ego mind tried to tell me that it was just my imagination. Eventually I ignored the ego part of me and listened to what the Universe was telling me.

During the beginning phase, unintentionally, I found a way to drive my Angels and Spirit Guides "crazy." I was so excited with this new-found talent. Each day I would think of a million things to ask for during that night's meditation. But by the time I sat down to meditate, I had eliminated just about everything because I felt these requests weren't important enough. As with Aladdin's Lamp, I thought that you only receive three wishes, and I didn't want to waste any. One night, a very strong, firm voice came through and said: "Barbara, there is no limit on how much you can ask for, you just have to ASK!" I'm not sure, but I think they may be sorry they shared that tidbit of information as I now ask constantly, not just for myself, but for others who are also in need.

On a Thanksgiving morning more than twenty years ago, while taking a hot leisurely bath, I mentally expressed my thanks to God for all my blessings. Upon finishing, I heard a male voice in the room (not the usual voice in my head). This startled me and even though I could not see anyone, I scrambled to use the nine inch square face cloth to cover my "private" parts. Needless to say, it didn't quite cover everything. The voice said: "My Child, I am here in answer to your prayer to Our Father." It was Jesus. I did not know that He was on my team of spiritual advisors committed to helping me accomplish my Soul's purpose.

In time Jesus asked that I call him "Sananda." Again, as an ex-Catholic, saying this was hard, but I finally became comfortable calling Jesus by His Oversoul name — "Sananda!" In this book you will notice that sometimes I make reference to Jesus and sometimes to Sananda. I do this not to confuse you, but to reference the entity which gave me the information. Jesus usually comes when my energy is at a low point, as He is operating as an individual energy. When he comes as Sananda, He is operating from the Oversoul (group) energy, which is much more powerful.

Getting onto and staying on one's spiritual path is not always easy, especially if we still have to operate in the so-called "normal" or everyday world. The more I connected with the spiritual world the more uncomfortable my "normal" world became. I had my ups and downs and at times wanted to give up. I was fortunate enough to have excellent guidance that gave me some breathing space, but eventually Spirit tapped me on the shoulder and said it's time to get going again.

Even though I started out only lecturing on Angels, my spiritual guidance has expanded the number of topics I talk about — all are self-help spiritual programs and include:

- ✳ Connecting/Healing/Manifesting with Your Angels
- ✳ Meditation
- ✳ Path of the Soul/Reincarnation
- ✳ Soul Purpose/Life Mission
- ✳ Spiritual Fitness/Growth
- ✳ Ascension

- ✳ Past Life Regression
- ✳ Stress Control
- ✳ Spirit Attachment/Releasement
- ✳ Sugar Addiction

Regarding Ascension, my Angels led me to Dr. Joshua David Stone's book *The Complete Ascension Manual* before I was ready for it. Opened it, thumbed through it, and then put it aside for two years. When I went back to it, I read it from cover to cover, but didn't absorb much. Then I read it a second time and something inside of me clicked. It became so clear and made perfect sense.

About twelve years ago, I started offering classes on Ascension, but was not successful in attracting attendees. So I called Dr. Stone's office to see if he would be willing to come out to New England and do an Ascension Workshop. His assistant said he was not lecturing publicly. He was working full-time at the academy he established in California. Within a very short time she called me back, said she had spoken to Dr. Stone about my call, and he invited me to come to California for a Wesak (Buddhist) Festival he was sponsoring in Mt. Shasta and asked that I stay a day longer and be a part of his World Leaders and Teachers Conference.

This one-day conference was by invitation only. I was floating on top of the clouds when I hung up, but again FEAR set in. I called her back and told her I was honored to be invited to the special conference, but I was not a World Leader or Teacher, just a "local." She laughed and said that Joshua was guided by above and that he would not have invited me if I were not supposed to be there. I went that year in 2000 and for the next four years. While I was personally saddened when Joshua was called back to the Spirit World in 2005, this subject has become one of my passions. I reach up and express thanks to Joshua for introducing me to the Path of Ascension.

We are fortunate to be on Earth at this special time in history. Earth is ascending from the 3rd to the 4th Dimension and then to the 5th Dimension. We, too, are ascending from 3rd to 4th to 5th and some will even reach the 6th dimensional level of vibration during this lifetime. Our DNA contains keys and codes that are automatically triggered to assist us in our spiritual awakening and evolution. The energy shifts of 2012 will accelerate the awakening for many. It is time for us to embrace this wonderful opportunity and the "real" reason we came to Earth.

Remember, you are NOT alone on this journey. Do not struggle with life. We have a great deal of assistance available, not only on the earth plane, but we also have a host of advisors assigned to help from the spirit world. It's all part of our birthright as a human.

Please keep in mind that I am a channel for Spirit to be able to present information to humanity from a spiritual perspective. Please do not take offense to any of what may seem like controversial issues presented in *Creating Heaven on Earth*, as that is definitely not the intention. During the process of Ascension, it is important that we view circumstances through our spiritual eyes, which will make things much clearer. We are all working towards the same goals — to increase our Light, expand our capacity to Love, return to Oneness, and create Heaven/Peace on Earth.

God Bless you all!

Editor's Note

While the author may refer to "God" with the human construct of "He," the author recognizes and firmly believes that God and Source are energy, without gender, as are all humans in spirit form.

PART I

CREATION
AND
PATH OF THE SOUL

Chapter 1

WHO CREATED GOD?

As a child I learned that God created us. I did not question this fact. However, as an adult I became curious as to who created God. Could he have created himself?

In my "search" for the answer, all I could find from traditional religious sources was the theory that God did not need to be created as He was All That Is and was self-created. For some reason, the question kept coming into my consciousness as the traditional explanation was not sitting well with me.

Many years ago while meditating and believing I had connected with the energy known as Jesus, I asked the question: "Who created God?" I assumed if anyone knew the answer to this question it would be Jesus.

This was His response: "There are many Gods." Hearing that answer, I was sure that somehow I had connected with darkness (not Jesus) as I had been warned by my teachers when I first started channeling that the darkness would try to come in through the names of high level spiritual beings. Believing that everyone knew there was only one God, I shut my meditation down and didn't bring that question up again — until recently.

One God for Each Universe

A few years ago, knowing Jesus as Sananda, I asked the question again: "Who created God?" The response this time was: "There are multi-millions of Gods." Knowing it was Sananda, not the darkness or my ego giving me this information, I asked him to explain what he meant by that statement.

Sananda explained that the Source created one God to head up each of the Universes that were in existence at that time. While it is true that there is only one God in charge of the Universe where Earth is located, it was time for us to open our awareness that we were in the process of becoming multi-dimensional beings and to know there were other Gods and Universes in existence other than the one associated with Earth. Also, it is the Source's long-range plan for us to become Gods and to be able to create our own Universes.

One Source

My next question to Sananda, after getting a satis-factory explanation of who created God, was: "If Source created God, then who created Source?" A smile came across my face when Sananda responded: "We will save that question for another time." Sananda probably felt since it took me so long to accept this tidbit of informa-tion, that He would give me time to digest it before giving me more. My intuition tells me that the Great Central Sun is SOURCE; however, this has not been confirmed nor denied by my spiritual guidance at this time.

Chapter 2

SOUL CREATION, THE FALLEN ANGELS, FREE WILL AND REINCARNATION

WHEN THE SOURCE WANTED TO EXPERIENCE life in the outer worlds, the lower vibrating dimensions, and bring Light to this territory, the Gods from all Universes were called together to brainstorm and determine how that could be done.

It was decided that a spark of Source energy would be prepared for travel to Earth to experience all there is to experience and then return Home to the higher dimensions. This spark of Source Light was infused into an incubator-type device similar to a honeycomb. When the gestation period was complete, the new Soul was assigned to a family/group that would parent the Soul and prepare it for its journey to Earth.

There has been a joke-type story around for years as to where the Soul for humans should be placed on Earth. I do not know who the original author is, but I have seen many different versions. The one I remember goes something like this: When God created the human, he called his Angels together and asked where would be the best place to hide the TRUTH about who they were. One Angel suggested hiding it at the top of the highest mountain. Another Angel suggested the best place to hide it would be at the bottom of the deepest ocean. A third Angel said NO! NO! NO! You need to hide the TRUTH deep within them for they will never find it there.

We Are Spiritual Beings

I guess there's more truth than fiction to this story as we are now just awakening to the fact that we are special spiritual beings and have all the answers, love and every-thing we need within us. We have spent many lifetimes, and part of this one, looking outside of ourselves for the answers. Life is so much easier when we take some quiet time to go within and ask for what we want and need and then not worry about the outcome.

We came into human form with the spark of Divine Light within to help guide us along the best possible path for learning and growing. Once we get beyond the ego self, connect with our Soul Self and then with our

Higher Self, the spiritual part of us that resides on the other side, life is really good! This all happens through our experiences.

Before the Creation of the Physical Body

Originally, before the creation of the human body, the earth was occupied by non-physical spiritual beings. Amelius, part of the Jesus/Sananda energy and one of the non-physical beings, reported to God that a spiritual body in a physical world was not working. There was no spiritual growth or evolution happening. It was then that God (not Source) created the human body. There have been revisions to it over the years, such as the Neanderthal and caveman outer bodies, and there will be additional changes in the future. The major change going on right now is the transformation of our inner body from a carbon-based to a crystalline (Light) body. While this change cannot be seen, it can be felt during the transformation period through physical pain, and afterwards by the rise in our consciousness. There is also the expansion of the stomach area referred to as the Buddha Belly. This is being created to add additional glands and organs in that area of the body to store more oxygen to accommodate the increased Light body in future lifetimes. If you are eating healthy and exercising and still have an extended stomach, don't worry, it's all part of the process of Ascension. Even today, when the physical body ceases to function, if the Soul stays earth-bound, there is no further growth for the Soul.

We Are Gods-in-Training

The spark of Divine Light that occupies each of us humans is Source Light, and the God of our Universe is also Source Light. We are Gods-in-training. Others who have come before us have already achieved this level and are now assisting us in our journey to higher realms. It is a wonderful time to be on Earth during the time of these energy shifts. There is more opportunity for spiritual growth than we have ever experienced before in the history of Earth.

Our purpose as humans is to grow to higher spiritual levels by opening our awareness of who we really are spiritually and expanding to higher vibrational levels through our thoughts, actions and deeds. And, by increasing the amount of Light we carry in our physical bodies, our spiritual vibration will automatically rise to higher levels, and we will have the opportunity to create our own Universes in the future.

The planet Earth was created by God (not Source). The original intention was for this to be a physical world where we could eventually create Heaven on Earth, and it would be our responsibility to bring this plan to fruition. The two shifts of energy, Earth's Alignment and the peak of the Galactic Shift, both happening in 2012 will bring us much closer to this reality.

MONADS, OVERSOULS, AND EXTENSIONS

According to Dr. Joshua David Stone, God created 60,000 million Monads for Planet Earth described as angelic masses of energy, which branch into twelve off-shoots called Oversouls. Each Oversoul branches into an additional twelve offshoots called Extensions. We are an Extension. Each time we come to Earth, learn our lessons through life experiences and then return Home, we grow spiritually. When we reach a certain level of vibration, we meld back into the energy of the Oversoul, which Jesus and many others have already done. At this point we no longer operate as individuals; we operate as a cluster or group of souls, which is a much more powerful vibration. When all the Oversouls reach a certain level of vibration, they will return back to the Monad. We still have plenty of time to complete this mission.

The Fallen Angels

Who are the Fallen Angels? We are — all of humanity! Some people believe there are only a few "bad apples" that chose to go against God and, therefore, were cast out of Heaven and are making life miserable for the rest of us. This is part of the illusion.

Past Life Regression therapy will reveal that we all have had lifetimes where we performed "evil" type acts, such as murder, torture, slander, rape, etc. This is how karma came into being. When we returned "Home" and went through our Life Review, we saw and felt how our thoughts, actions and deeds hurt others and decided that we would schedule similar experiences to go through ourselves in a future life to balance things out. This is not a punishment by God. God does not punish us. We (humanity) made the decision that we would learn and grow through the process of pain and suffering — a form of self-inflicted punishment that would raise us to a higher vibration.

VOLUNTEERING FOR SPIRITUAL GROWTH

The truth is that when God created Earth and found that life in spiritual form did not work on a physical planet, He went to the 7th Dimension and asked His Angels if any of them wanted to volunteer for this mission. He explained that the purpose of this experiment of life in physical form was to grow to higher spiritual levels and allow the Source to experience and bring Light to the outer worlds through us. He also reminded us that we would be giving up a great deal, as life on Earth in physical form would not be easy. We would "forget" who we were as spiritual beings. We would be given a precious gift of Free Will to make decisions for ourselves, so that, individually, we could grow at our own pace based on our decisions.

The movie *City of Angels* depicts the Fallen Angel situation beautifully. Nicholas Cage, the Angel assigned to watch over Meg Ryan, the surgeon, fell in love with her and wanted to spend time with her in the physical world. In order to do this, he had to "fall" from the higher realms. When I saw this movie for the first time, I wondered how many people got the message that was so obvious to me. Whenever I held one of my Angel workshops, I would ask the attendees if they had seen the movie and if they got the message. Most did not. While we tend to think of anything coming out of Hollywood as made up fiction, there is truth in this story.

"AMNESIA" ON PLANET EARTH

We were all angelic beings and when we volunteered to come to Earth in physical form to have our experiences and to grow to higher levels, we all had to descend ("fall") from the 7th Dimension to the 3rd Dimension — a much denser vibration for sure. We got caught up in our physicality and forgot about our spirituality. This is referred to as the "amnesia effect."

It was very difficult to get "unstuck" from the 3rd Dimension. But many have accomplished this challenge and are now reaching even higher levels. Many have incarnated in this lifetime at a higher vibration in order to bring greater Light to the Planet during this special time in our history. Earth's Alignment in 2012, which happens approximately every 26,000 years, occurs at approximately the mid-point of the Galactic Shift which happens approximately every 100-110 million years. Our rate of growth will be much faster and easier from this point forward.

Free Will

We have Free Will while in Spirit form in the higher dimensions. This special gift was given to those of us who chose to come to Earth. While God had good intentions with His gift of Free Will, our misuse of it has created many of our struggles. Instead of using it for the good or betterment of ourselves and our fellow humans, we chose to use it in ways that were destructive to ourselves as well as the Planet.

Free Will as an Illusion

When I first received the message from Spirit that Free Will was part of the illusion, it made me stop and think. Finally it dawned on me that, if we make our decisions from our Heart (Soul) center with good intentions, we usually experience positive results and emotions. However, when we make our decisions from our head or ego, based in any way on deception, greed, manipulation, revenge, or control, then we experience negative results and emotions. In the end, after experiencing all there is to experience, we should have learned through our many lifetimes that making the decisions from our Heart/Soul center causes us to feel better, and we grow to higher spiritual levels.

Free Will as a Tool and Teacher

So if decisions from our Heart and Soul make us feel good and help us to grow, and decisions made from a negative perspective cause us pain, suffering and karma, where's the Free Will? Free Will is a tool and teacher to help guide us to our authentic self. This is the point we are at now, and this will lead us to Ascended Master status. So use your Free Will wisely.

Misuse of Free Will

As an example, I would like to share one instance of my misuse of Free Will. Many years ago when I first started on my spiritual path, I had the luxury of a connection with my Spirit Guides and Angels. I was working in the corporate world at that time and experienced a lot of stress. I learned from a fellow associate that someone in the company had told a lie about me. My fellow associate thought that what he heard didn't sound right. It didn't sound like something I would do so he came to me and gave me an opportunity to explain. I was livid.

Ordinarily I would have confronted the individual who told the lie, but because I had promised I would keep our conversation confidential, I was not able to do anything about it. I could have let it go and been satisfied with the opportunity to set the record straight. But, no, mentally I was plotting a "get even" event. My Spirit Guide knew what I was considering and advised that it would not be in my highest best interest to do as I was "thinking." I overrode that advice, exercised my Free Will, and went ahead with my plan.

The individual who told the lie about me was having a bad day. Knowing he was at a low point, I went in for the "kill" and made his life even more miserable. He ended up going home early because he couldn't take any more.

I was feeling pretty good, powerful, thinking that I had gotten even. Within a few hours that feeling passed. A friend of mine happened to call. She said something to me that hurt me and when I hung up, I started to cry — something very unusual for me in the workplace. I realized that my friend had no idea how her "innocent" comment affected me. She did not intend to hurt my feelings. I knew that it was the Universe's way of allowing me the experience of feeling how I "intentionally" caused someone else to feel only a few short hours beforehand.

A Lesson Learned Well

"What goes around comes around." That was a lesson learned well. I now know that it is so much easier to let anger and frustration go and to forgive others than to carry out revengeful or negative actions. Life is good!

Reincarnation

The original plan for humanity did not include rein-carnation. The plan was to have one physical lifetime that would encompass thousands of years before our return to Spirit. However, reincarnation became neces-sary as a result of our descent from the 7th Dimension to the 3rd Dimension, now referred to as the "Fall." Through hindsight it is obvious that one lifetime was not enough time for us to accomplish bringing Heaven to Earth. There was too much to do.

CHANGES IN OUR VIBRATION

When God asked for volunteers to experience physi-cal life on this wonderful planet called Earth, we were supposed to come down, experience everything there was to experience, and then return home to the other side. Because the drop in energy vibration from 7th Dimension to 3rd Dimension was so great, we forgot who we were, got stuck and believed that we were only human and not spiritual beings. The "Fall" changed our vibration so that we were not able to return to the 7th Dimension. Upon physical death, we ended up in an interim location called the Astral Plane, a place between the two worlds of Earth and Spirit.

From the Astral Plane we were able to return to

Earth over and over again to learn and grow spiritually until such time as we reached the 5th level of vibration. In the past very few Souls were able to master achieving this higher vibration.

MORE SPIRITUALLY EVOLVED SOULS

At this special time in Earth's history, many Souls have evolved enough so that they can return to the higher realms (5th and 6th Dimensions) and bypass the Astral Plane. Even now, we cannot return to the other side without an escort from the Light. We can't make it on our own because of the density of our energy from a gravity planet.

Have you noticed that the majority of Souls from each new generation are wiser and more spiritually evolved? Many of our children, grandchildren, and great grandchildren are arriving at a higher spiritual vibration. Many at such a high level do not need to incarnate any longer because of the level they have achieved, but they have decided to come to Earth to make life easier for us and to assist the planet in rising to higher levels.

PAST LIFE REGRESSION

At one time, I did not believe in reincarnation. However, when I took my hypnosis training, Past Life Regression Therapy was part of it. No one asked or was concerned whether you believed in past lives or not.

Much to my surprise, once I started accessing past life memories from my subconscious mind, I was amazed to learn that some of the events going on in my life were associated with past life issues I had brought forward to work on and release in this lifetime. Life is easier when you understand what is going on and why you are going through different and often difficult situations. We bring those issues which we did not complete in our past lives forward to complete in order to grow to higher spiritual levels.

Chapter 3

PREPARATION FOR OUR JOURNEY TO EARTH

WE DO A LOT OF PREPARATION WORK WHILE in the Spirit World before we incarnate. However, we have a lot of help in making our choices. We also have Free Will while in Spirit so we can discard the advice we receive from our spiritual helpers. While it would be in our highest best interest to follow the advice of our counselors, as they know better than we do, it is our experience so we have the ultimate say as to what we will choose to do during each incarnation.

After a decision is made to enter physical form, we go through a number of steps before actually incarnating. We select our Spirit Guides, the lessons for us to learn, our Guardian Angels, our gender, body type and personality, location and nationality, and other Souls in our contract. Often we go through a dress rehearsal and are finally escorted to Earth.

Even though we make agreements with other Souls, and the agreements are placed in our Soul Contract/ Blueprint, sometimes these contracts are broken. Many times these broken contracts relate to miscarriage, still-birth, crib death (Sudden Infant Death Syndrome) and abortion. Adoption does not result from a broken contract; it is part of your original contract and Spirit wanted to share information on these issues.

When all these situations are viewed from a spiritual perspective, you will notice that everything that happens contributes to our spiritual growth.

Selection of Spirit Guides

These wonderful Light Beings, along with members of our Heavenly Council, a Council consisting of 12 Ascended Masters and one Archangel, help us in determining who and what to include in our upcoming incarnation. Spirit Guides have been in physical form and have decided to assist us along our spiritual path as we journey from the Spirit World to Earth. We know them from either our Soul Group or through other physical incarnations.

When I was in fourth grade history class, the teacher talked about Captain John Smith and Pocahontas. There was a picture of them in our textbook. That picture made such an impression on me. My body was covered in goosebumps, but at that young age, I didn't understand what was going on. Today, many years later, I can still see the picture from the textbook in my mind's eye.

While taking mediumship classes at the church where I am now ordained, I struggled whether or not I was actually making a connection with Spirit. The instructor told us to tell our guides how we wanted them to communicate with us. So I mentally put out the request that I wanted to have a telepathic two-way conversation with them as I would if they were here physically. Suddenly, in my head, I heard a male voice from the Spirit World identify himself as Jonathan, my Master Guide, and that I would know him from history as Captain John Smith. I guess that's why his picture in the history book from fourth grade made such an impression on me. At some level I "knew" him and that we would be working together. He has had to exercise a lot of tolerance and patience with me as I think I was "Doubting Thomas" in a past life.

Lessons

Before we incarnate we determine what we want to accomplish and what lessons we want to bring forward to work on. We can refer to our Life Book of Records to see what still has to be completed. Sometimes we start a lesson in one lifetime and, if we are not able to complete it, it will be carried over to a future life. When we schedule a lesson that is partially completed, it is much easier to get through in the upcoming lifetime.

Selection of Guardian Angels

Guardian Angels have never had a physical life, but are more than willing to serve us from the Angelic Realm — that is their sole purpose. They volunteer for the assignment of being our Guardian Angels and we select, from these volunteers, the ones we want to work with. Every human has at least one Guardian Angel, most have two. According to Jesus, the maximum number of Guardian Angels that can be assigned to a human is five. In the case of Guardian Angels, less is better.

From a human perspective, I felt cheated when I learned I only had two Guardian Angels. I was doing God's work, so I thought I should have the five. I was told "you do not want five, as more is not better." Jesus explained that the more Guardian Angels assigned to an individual is an indication of a very difficult Life Plan. When I asked Him for an example of someone I might know who was assigned five, thinking it might be a Pope or other religious figure, I was told that Hitler had five. I am now more than satisfied with my two wonderful Guardian Angels.

Depending upon how difficult the lessons are in our Life Plan, we are assigned a number of Guardian

Angels to help us, and we get to choose them from the volunteers who come forward on our behalf. You don't always have the same Guardian Angels lifetime after lifetime. The two that I have in this lifetime have been with me in other lifetimes, but not all other lifetimes. While in Spirit we do not have a gender — we are energy. For the purpose of helping us in the best possible way, Angels take on a gender vibration. I have both a male and a female Guardian Angel. However, I have read for individuals who have all male or all female Angels working with them.

Gender

Whom do you want to be — a male or female? This is usually determined by what lessons you have chosen. Sometimes it is easier to accomplish what you want as a female than it would be as a male. When looking at your Life Book of Records, if you see that you scheduled a lesson as a female and you did not succeed, then you might want to try it as a male. You have had lifetimes as both males and females.

Choose a Body Type and Personality

Select a physical body to suit your purpose. For instance, if you wanted to be a sumo wrestler, you would not choose the same type of body as a race horse jockey. During the planning stage your Soul has an opportunity to "slip into" different body types in order to feel what is most comfortable. When I share this information in my lectures, the general response is: "What was I thinking when I chose this body!" We may have chosen our bodies on the other side, but what we do with them when we're down here makes the difference.

Also, what we choose to do in life determines the type of personality we choose. If you are planning to be a salesperson or motivational speaker, a more outgoing, dynamic, charismatic personality would suit you best.

Geographical Location and Nationality

Where do you want to be in the world? Again, this has to do with what we want to accomplish. We may decide to start out in one area and then move to a different part of the country or world in the same lifetime.

Agreements with Other Souls in Our Life Plan

Next we select and meet our parents, other important family members and individuals who will help us achieve our goals. Even if these individuals, who will be part of our life, are already in physical form, we may meet with their Higher Self, the Spirit part of their being, to make these agreements, or their Soul can journey to the other side from the physical plane during sleep or rest time. The Soul travels to the other side every night during sleep time so that would be a very natural thing to do. We discuss the part they will play in assisting us to learn and grow, and then make our agreements. This is a two-way street. We also agree to help others with their lessons. Usually when there are significant relationships in a Life Plan, it is for the purpose of both individuals learning from each other.

A Special Message Regarding Adoption

For those who have had the experience of being an adoptee, here is the spiritual guidance given to me: Let go of the hurt, anger, and rejection from this experience. Your biological mother agreed to be the pathway for you to enter the physical world. It was meant for someone else to be a parental figure in your life to help you learn your lessons and grow spiritually. Be thankful you are here and be thankful for the parents who loved you enough to bring you into their life and provide for you. We all want to feel loved and wanted, but the most important thing is to make the most of the time we have here on Earth to learn and grow.

As an example, St. Germain tells me that Francis Bacon's biological mother was Queen Elizabeth I. She did not want him and was going to have him put to death. Lady Bacon, a staff member for Queen Elizabeth, said that she would take him and raise him as her own. Queen Elizabeth agreed. At age 12 Francis Bacon intuitively knew that Queen Elizabeth was his biological mother and confronted her with this information. She confirmed it was correct, but threatened to have him put to death if he told anyone. Francis Bacon achieved Ascended Master status in that lifetime. We know this Soul today as St. Germain.

What St. Germain wanted me to convey is that it doesn't matter who brought you into the world, it's what you do when you get here that counts. Don't allow the fact that you are adopted become a stumbling block to achieving your mission. This is the most important lifetime for humans in Earth's history so do the best you can.

Soul Contracts

Once agreements are made, they are entered into our Soul contracts. At the right time these individuals will enter our life and will assist us unconsciously with whatever their contract calls for. Many times, if it is seen that you have to deal with a very challenging aspect, others may be assigned to step in and assist when the contract for the first individual is up or the contracts could overlap.

While I was doing a Soul Purpose reading for a woman, she expressed concern that she was not able to help a friend who was going through a tough time. The reading revealed that her contract with her friend had ended and that her friend would be connected with another individual to help with that same lesson. This does not mean failure. It only means that we are scheduled to be with individuals for a certain period of time and when our time is up we need to move on.

If you are not happy with the individuals in your life, know that you chose them. Learning lessons is not easy. Shift your perspective of these individuals from mean, cruel, nasty, etc., to "they are helping me to grow spiritually and I thank them." It will make life easier both for you and them when you reach this point.

Dress Rehearsal

Many times before we come to Earth, we go through a dress rehearsal with significant individuals so that we will recognize them when it is time to connect with them on Earth. Usually there is something unique about the individual that we study and ingrain into our subconscious minds that will attract us when we meet the individual in physical life. You can step into a scene of your life to see how you will handle important events. I used to think déjà vu had to do with memories of a past life. This may be true, but it could also be remembrance from our dress rehearsal.

Good-Bye

Next we say good-bye to our fellow Soul group members.

Gateway to Earth

Our Spirit Guides, chosen before we come into physical form, escort us to the portal/gateway for entry to Earth when it is time for us to descend.

Soul Connection with the Physical Body

The Soul can enter the physical body at any time from conception up to three months after birth. The Soul usually visits the body, but most Souls wait until close to birthing or after birth to enter the physical body as the womb is too confining.

The entire Soul energy does not enter the physical body all at once. Approximately every seven years, as the physical body advances in age, an additional amount of Soul energy joins the human through age twenty-one. By age twenty-one you have all the Soul energy needed for your experience. This is all part of the contract made before incarnation.

Soul Decides Not to Enter Physical Body

If the Soul decides not to enter the physical body even after the three month period, the physical body will pass. This sometimes happens in what we call "crib death" or SIDS (Sudden Infant Death Syndrome). Also should the Soul decide not to enter the physical body or not yet be ready for the physical life before birth, the mother will experience what we call a miscarriage or a stillborn child depending upon the stage of pregnancy when the Soul decides not to enter. The decision not to enter physical life could be part of the contract for learning a life lesson or for karma purposes. We don't fully understand what we put into our agreements before incarnating, but there is ALWAYS a spiritual reason why things are happening as they are.

Abortion

Just as the Soul has opportunities to exit its contract if it does not feel ready to have the experience of being in a physical body, the mother has the same right to exit her contract through abortion. While I am not in favor of this method, and I personally believe other choices would be more appropriate, Spirit wanted me to share this information with those who have made this decision in order to ease any feelings of guilt and "beating up" on oneself. On a spiritual level, it is important to forgive oneself and others, and move on.

While abortion may appear to be a quick fix to an immediate problem, there are other aspects to be considered. For example, 1) the emotional, psychological effects of guilt and remorse; 2) physical effect of possibly not being able to get pregnant at a future time when conditions are more stable in one's life; and 3) relationship of the father with the child. Many men are not given the option as to whether or not they want the baby to be a part of their life.

The Soul will find another time or avenue to enter into physical life. According to Spirit, when the mother decides not to fulfill its contract with the incoming Soul, the Soul experiences a feeling of disappointment, such as when a child is told they cannot have a piece of candy before dinner.

Birth Control

Abortion should definitely NOT be used as a form of birth control. There are better methods available to us. If traditional birth control fails, one option for the mother who finds herself considering abortion might be to think of birthing the baby and allowing a couple who wants children, but are not able to conceive, the opportunity to love and provide for this little one through adoption.

My contract called for me to give birth to two children in this lifetime — a boy and a girl. Naturally I was not consciously aware of this, but did practice birth control. I only have one child — a wonderful son. The female Soul I was scheduled to bring forward is now in my life as my granddaughter. I am enjoying her so much. She is truly an advanced Soul and will probably be my teacher when she gets older.

Letting Go of Right and Wrong

In the next chapter we will discuss life in physical form and learning our lessons. It is time for humanity to adjust our thinking and let go of the right and wrong of any situation. No matter what is happening, no matter how difficult life appears to be, individually and collectively through changing our perspective and thinking and acting spiritually, we have the power to change our circumstances.

Chapter 4

PHYSICAL LIFE — LEARNING LESSONS

LIFE IS ALL ABOUT "LESSONS"— LEARNING
through our experiences brought about by our Free
Will decisions, and growing to a higher spiritual vibration. When we were planning for this physical lifetime,
we chose the lessons we wanted to experience and the
people who would help us with them. Our Soul Plan/
Mission is embedded in our DNA and circumstances
happen as they are programmed in our blueprint. In my
Soul Purpose readings, I have found that most individuals carry three major lessons in their Life Plan. A few
individuals may only have one or two major lessons, but
everyone is here to learn and grow spiritually. At this

time in Earth's history, many Ascended Masters have chosen to incarnate to assist us and the Earth on our journey to the higher realms. They, too, are continuing to learn and grow. The only difference is they don't have to deal with the karma as we do.

Karma can be good or bad. Good Karma is experienced as a reward for past life actions and deeds which resulted in spiritual growth. Bad Karma isn't really "bad"— it is the balancing of our actions or deeds performed in past lives or possibly in our current life which we are not proud of or did not result in spiritual growth. Things are speeding up as a result of the energy being downloaded to Earth so we have an opportunity to balance things quickly. Forgiveness is an excellent tool in balancing Karma.

When my grandson was only a few weeks old, I was holding and rocking him as he fell asleep. He looked so sweet and innocent. I reached up and my prayer to God was to keep him safe, and only let him have positive and good experiences in life. My Spirit Guides and Angels immediately said, "NO, you don't want that!" I insisted that I wanted the very best for him and for him to have a stress-free easy life would be the very best. My Guides and Angels, once again, insisted that would not be in HIS highest best interest. I then remembered that we are here to learn and grow, and without the challenges for us to face and overcome there is no purpose for being here.

I immediately revised my prayer to protect and watch over him and help him learn what he is here to learn in the most graceful way possible.

Three Personal Lessons

Learning lessons is not easy until we reach the state of awareness of who we are. Then, when we encounter the struggles of life, we usually recognize there is something to be learned from each situation, and we work with our spiritual guides to help us get through what we are here to learn. This makes life a lot easier.

As an example, I would like to share three personal life lessons with you. This is not for the purpose of anyone feeling sorry for me or thinking my ex-husband is a "bad" guy, but to demonstrate how shifting our perception of situations from the human 3rd Dimension to the spiritual 5th Dimension can make all the difference in the world.

We had been married for forty years. It was a seesaw marriage of emotional ups and downs, but there was love at the base, which made the down times tolerable. He was a flirtatious-type of guy which enraged me in the beginning of our marriage. The lesson he was teaching me through his actions was *Jealousy.*

Long story short, I caught him in an affair and while driving to a lawyer's office to file for divorce, my Spirit Guide said, "No, Barbara. It would be in your highest best interest to stay in this relationship."

At that time, I could see absolutely no reason how staying in the relationship could have benefitted me one bit. However, I had learned to trust my Spirit Guides, as they had proven to me that they were looking out for me. The problem is they don't always explain the WHY of the situation. You have to trust. So, I turned around and headed back to this so-called unforgiveable relationship. With the help of my spiritual guidance I was able to forgive him. In time, I realized that the lesson he was helping me with in this case was actually **Forgiveness.**

Then the ultimate lesson arrived. I had been diagnosed with Rheumatoid Arthritis in the severest sense. On a scale of 1 to 10, 10 being the worst case scenario, I was a 10+. My family, friends and anyone who knew me thought I was going to die. I had lost a lot of weight and could hardly move. I could not even close my hand to open a door, to turn on the water faucets, or open anything. My husband had to run my bath water, comb my hair and assist me in getting dressed. I was totally dependent upon him. I was too sick and in too much pain to see the signs that were so obvious to everyone else. He was involved in another affair. When I started to feel a little better, these signs became very obvious to me. I asked my Spirit Guides to help bring the affair out in the open and this time I would not turn back. I went through all the human emotions — anger, hatred, hurt, depression, etc. Again, time is a wonderful healer, as I learned that the lesson he was helping me with in this situation was **Unconditional Love.**

I am grateful for having gone through all of these experiences, especially Unconditional Love. While it may seem happenstance, it was all programmed in our DNA. We had a certain length of time to be together and to learn what we needed to learn, and it was time to move on and have other experiences with other individuals. I have not only forgiven him, but released him from blame, and I am fortunate to be able to call him a friend now. I can honestly say I love him, but in a different way. I love him the way God loves all of us, not the romantic or sexual kind of love. It feels really good not to feel all those negative emotions that I felt in the beginning of the breakup of our marriage. Forgiveness does not mean that you have to return to a situation that was uncomfortable. It only releases you from the burden of carrying those negative emotions and allowing them to raise havoc with your mind, body and spirit. Let them go. They serve no valuable purpose, no purpose at all except destruction on any or all levels — physical, emotional, mental and spiritual.

Placement of Life Lessons

What I have learned about the order of our Life Lessons is that they are placed before us in the order we put them in our Life Plan. For example, I would not have been able to work on Unconditional Love as the first or second lesson. Once I completed Jealousy, I had many years before I started on Forgiveness. Then I had approximately ten years before the Unconditional Love lesson was placed before me. Lessons build on each other.

Even though I had connected with my Spirit Guides at the time I started going through my lessons, I didn't fully understand what was going on, except for the fact that life was difficult, and I was unhappy most of the time. Once I completed the Unconditional Love lesson, it was revealed to me what I had spent my time going through. During meditation one evening, I connected with my Master Guide, Jonathan, and he gave me a Life Review meditation exercise to use in my classes in helping individuals to know how well they were doing spiritually while on Earth. I went through the exercise to see what type of information would be revealed. I was surprised that the first lesson (Jealousy) was more difficult and took longer to get through than the last lesson (Unconditional Love). The reason for this is that I was at a lower vibration, and as I worked through the lessons and raised my vibration, the lessons got easier.

It is possible to be almost complete with one lesson and then circumstances will be brought forward to help you get started on the next lesson. A word of caution, the more times a lesson has to be placed before you, the more difficult it becomes. The consequences of "not getting it" are more severe. As an example, my son had an automobile accident as a result of reckless driving and totaled the vehicle. The car was insured and replaced. Physically he only got a scratch which needed a band-aid. He didn't learn the lesson with that experience. Within a short period of time, approximately two years later, he had another accident under very similar circumstances. This time he lost $10,000 as the vehicle was not insured, and he had physical damage to his body and needed two operations. While driving him to the hospital, I told him that he better learn the lesson being placed before him as the next time he might be responsible for killing himself or someone else in a car accident. Thank God he has not had any accidents in the last eighteen years.

If you have a lesson programmed to experience, the Universe will set up circumstances for as long as it takes to help you learn what you have decided you wanted to learn in this lifetime. For instance, if I was not in constant contact with my spiritual guidance, I would not have heard them tell me to turn back from the lawyer's office. I would have gotten the divorce at that time. But then I would have had to connect with another individual to learn this lesson. So I would have experienced heartache, pain and suffering again with someone else, and it would have destroyed my faith in relationships. By returning to the relationship, I had ten good years before it was time for my next lesson. When my Spirit Guides advised that it would be in my highest best interest to return to the relationship, I had made a "bargain" with them that if I caught my husband in another affair, there would be no turning back. At the time I did not know that was part of my Life Plan so everything worked out as it was supposed to. I share this information with you so that if you are experiencing ending one relationship after another, and you are experiencing the same type of situation only with different characters, know that there is something you need to learn before things can get better — and they do get better!

In our early experiences of incarnation on Earth, we only put one lesson in our Life Plan and most times did not complete it. It took many lifetimes to complete one lesson. Because of our evolution and the Earth's evolution and the energy shifts scheduled soon, we are now able to handle much more.

Regarding physical life, one thing to keep in mind is that, if you are feeling good about life and you are happy, chances are you are following your spiritual path. If you're not happy and life is a struggle, then you need to make some changes. When we resist change and stay with the same old, the same old things will not get better.

Revising Our Life Plan

Our Soul blueprint/contract is imbedded in our DNA and circumstances are brought into our life in order to deal with them and to grow spiritually as a result of moving through them. Even though we made these agreements/contracts on the other side, they are not set in concrete. They can be changed. As I mentioned before, we have Free Will in the Spirit World and sometimes we override the guidance that is provided to us because we "think" we can do it. When we get down here on Earth and find that it is too difficult, we are not stuck. We can ask our Spiritual Team if it is possible to make a revision to our Life Plan.

As an example, I had included "Loneliness in Old Age" to experience in this lifetime as I have scheduled almost 100 years before exiting. My Spirit Guides came to me through a friend and asked if they could change this part and eliminate it from my Life Plan as it was not necessary. I naturally agreed, and was surprised that I had included it. Who wants to be lonely in old age? Not me! Obviously I exercised my Free Will and overrode my Spiritual Team when originally creating my Life Plan. So I thank them for coming forward and giving me an opportunity to change what would have been a very unpleasant experience. If you are in the habit of meditating, ask your Spiritual Team if there is anything in your Life Plan that needs to be or can be changed.

Lessons for All of Humanity

In addition to individual Life Lessons, we sometimes volunteer to assist with lessons for all of humanity. These lessons happen at a level that our human minds cannot always understand. An example of this would be the O. J. Simpson, Nicole Brown-Simpson and Ronald Goldman situation. As I watched the police chase O.J.'s white Ford Bronco on TV, after the murder of Nicole and her friend Ronald Goldman, my guides gave me a heads up and said that he did it. I was surprised and shocked, because I liked O.J., but thought "what can I do?" I didn't know what my part in this situation would be until later. Even though my guides said, "He did it," I didn't feel any bitterness or hatred toward him. This is an advantage when working with Spirit. They knew he was fulfilling part of his contract so they held no malice toward him or his actions and transferred that energy to me when telling me that he committed this crime. I was amazed at how non-judgmental I was throughout the trial and even now. I never spent so much time watching TV as I did for this event.

My part with the O.J. situation would continue at a higher dimensional level. One night while meditating, I was very peaceful and just about to end the meditation when my body started to jerk in the chair, and I began to cry uncontrollably. This puzzled me as I did not feel sad and there was absolutely no reason for me to be carrying on like this. Soon I received the message — "He did it! He did it! He did it!" I had no idea who had come into my meditation, but my response was "Who did what?"

It was Nicole Brown Simpson. She said, "O.J. did it." I assured her that he was on trial and that justice would be served. She replied, "No it won't." From the higher realms they are able to see the outcome before it even happens on Earth.

The reason Nicole was escorted to me was for counseling so she could transition from the Resting Area (an interim place where Souls go when they are carrying a lot of negative energy) into the Light. Jesus and Archangel Michael had taught me how to assist Souls to the Light from the Resting Area. I asked her to invite Ronald Goldman to accompany her on her next visit to me so that they could go into the Light at the same time. During her next visit she came alone and said that Ronald didn't want to come. He did not believe what she was telling him about the necessity to release and let go of the negative energy in order to go to Heaven. So I proceeded with my counseling sessions with her until such time as she was ready to release and let go of the negativity she had accumulated on Earth. When she transitioned into the Light and didn't return to the Resting Area, Ronald finally came to me in meditation with a "show me" attitude and asked that I help him like I helped Nicole. He too transitioned shortly after he released the negativity he was carrying. Nicole and Ronald ended up in this interim location in order to release their burdens and have time for their Souls to heal before entering the Light and proceeding with whatever they would be assigned to do for the next part of their spiritual growth. Nicole had made one more visit to me after arriving in the Light and said that she was in the process of helping others who had died from spousal abuse as she had.

Even though it "appears" that O.J. got away with murder, there is a bigger picture. The three of them, O.J., Nicole, and Ronald had contracts and roles to play in order to awaken humanity that spousal abuse could no longer be tolerated. Until this trial, most states had weak laws about domestic abuse. They considered it a private issue and, if the spouse being abused didn't want to press charges, then the legal system had little recourse. According to Spirit, the only way to get this lesson across was through dramatic and traumatic situations with high profile individuals. Nicole's sister, Denise Brown, went on a crusade after Nicole's death and the laws are now changed. If the police are called in they can take action whether charges are pressed or not. President Clinton signed The Violence Against Women Act as part of the Violent Crime Control and Law Enforcement Act of 1994. Nicole's family established The Nicole Brown Foundation, which is dedicated to educating communities on domestic violence prevention.

Spirit explained that, if O.J. had received a prison sentence at that time, humanity would have been satisfied that he got what he deserved and that would have been the end of it. Many were outraged by him not going to prison for murder, but look at what O.J.'s life was like as a "free" man after the trial. The acquittal for O.J. was a much worse punishment than serving a sentence for murder.

The more humanity awakens to who they are and starts acting like spiritual beings, there will be less of a need for this type of lesson to take place. The ultimate sacrifice of life proved very successful in this lesson for humanity. When a news item captures national or international attention, know there is a lesson for the majority of humans to be learned.

Another example of a lesson for humanity was the Hitler situation. I was appalled to learn that the eternal Soul that called itself Hitler ascended to the Light. Jesus has such a gentle way of bringing things into a spiritual perspective for me. At one level I understand this; at another level it is beyond comprehension. I can only report what I have been allowed to perceive. Jesus explained that Hitler's mission was to help humanity to overcome the "fear" factor. Unfortunately, he failed. Had he succeeded, history would have been written very differently. I was asked to imagine how history would have changed if the majority of the multi-millions of Souls from the different ethnic groups and nationalities whom Hitler and his men were responsible for killing and torturing, had banded together and stood up to them. If that had happened, then Hitler's mission would have been successful. Hitler and his men would have been the victims. Instead, those multi-millions of Souls became paralyzed by their fear and ended up victims. I've been told by my Spirit Guides that it is not money that is the root of all evil — it's fear!

A more recent situation happened here in the U.S., when George W. Bush was President. I liked President Bush. I thought he was very personable and that he would do great things for our country. When it "appeared" that the country was in a downward spiral under his leadership, I asked Sananda what was going on. He indicated that President Bush was doing what he was supposed to be doing (according to his Life Plan), but we (Americans) were not doing our part.

I love working with Spirit as they hit you with stuff you don't see coming. Sananda explained that we, as Americans, were supposed to speak up in order to initiate change if we did not like what was going on. Instead most of us griped and complained that we didn't like things, but we didn't take a big enough stand. While individually we may feel we cannot do much, however, if we band together in sufficient numbers we can move mountains. One thing for sure, when President Bush returns to the other side, does his Life Review, and stands before his Council, he will witness spiritual growth for fulfilling his special role in this lesson.

The lesson is not over yet. There will be others placed in the President's seat, and we will need to monitor their progress. God had a plan for America — "The Land of The Free," — our democratic motto of a government for the people and by the people. We need to stand together, with at least the majority standing united, as there will always be pros and cons to every situation, and make our leaders accountable for their actions and decisions. We have grown accustomed to electing our leaders based on what they tell us in their campaigns that they will do when they become president. Unfortunately, many times when they get into office, they do whatever they want to or whatever they feel is popular at the time.

One thing I have learned, spiritually speaking, is that things are definitely not as they seem or appear to be. While we cannot always understand the workings of Spirit, it's time for us to realize that we are very powerful spiritual beings and we have absolutely nothing to fear, no matter how things "appear" to be. Keep in mind that what we fear is what we attract to ourselves. We have a connection with God, and by using that connection we are always safe no matter what is going on around us — no matter what happens.

Chapter 5

WHAT HAPPENS AFTER PHYSICAL DEATH?

FOR MOST PEOPLE DEATH REMAINS EITHER A great mystery or a fearful event. Therefore, my spiritual guidance has provided the following information in this chapter to help alleviate the fear of this very natural transition from physical back to spirit.

Death Is Good for the Soul

The Soul has gone through its experiences for this lifetime on Earth and now has an opportunity to return to a peaceful place. It is said that when a baby is born we rejoice; we celebrate the beginning of a new life, and the Angels cry as they know it will not be an easy road for this young one. Then the reverse happens when a human dies — we cry and the Angels rejoice and celebrate the return of the Soul home. As we grow to higher spiritual levels, we will be able to rejoice for our loved ones as they pass knowing that they are going to a better place. This is already happening on a small scale. Once you make the connection with the Spirit World, communication with your deceased loved ones will be easy; and they will confirm to you directly that life is much better for them. They are free of pain and struggle.

My mother and I had unresolved issues when she passed away. I was not on my spiritual path at that time, but when I learned how to meditate and communicate with Spirit, she and I had the best mother-daughter talk ever. We expressed regrets and forgiveness and she said she saw things differently from the other side and where she had made mistakes with me. She had seven children and tried her best to treat us all equally. However, I was "different." I had psychic abilities that neither of us knew about at that time and life seemed to be more of a struggle for me. After her Life Review she was able to see that I should have been treated "differently."

My father picked up the slack and tried to accommodate me the best that he could. One example is that I fought with my mother constantly while doing my homework as I needed to have the radio on very softly in order to concentrate. She did not understand how I could concentrate with the noise and insisted I study in complete silence. My father never interfered with her guidance over us, but he understood my situation and bought me a transistor radio with earphones. As a parent myself, I did the best I could, but now see the mistakes I made. I am very fortunate in that when I apologized to my son and asked for his forgiveness, he didn't have a clue what I was talking about. He has nothing but good memories of his childhood. Being an only child he did have certain advantages. Now he is a parent and I can see he is doing the best that he can. Each of us does the best we can and that is all that is expected — to do the best we can!

Our Escorts to the Spirit World

The Guardian Angels are assigned to escort the Soul back to the higher realms, to where the Souls are supposed to be depending upon their spiritual growth. If you incarnated at the 3rd dimensional vibration and grew to the 4th, 5th, or 6th vibration you cannot get there on your own. You need an escort from the Light. If it appears that the Soul will not go with the Angels, sometimes deceased loved ones or our Spirit Guides arrive to escort the Soul home.

Many humans believe that when we die, consciousness ceases as well. This is not true and is one of the main reasons why souls do not go with the Angels who are responsible to take them Home. As long as these Souls have consciousness, they believe they are still "alive" physically. We have three levels of consciousness — conscious mind, subconscious mind and super conscious mind. It is true that the conscious mind ceases to exist upon physical death. However, the subconscious and super conscious minds meld together and continue to operate. This is another reason why Souls do not go with the Angels who come to take them home. It takes a while to make the adjustment and the Angels can only stay a very short time (approximately ten minutes of earth time) if we choose not to go with them. Their assignment is done and they have to move on.

Those who have had Near Death Experiences can attest to the fact that, if it is not your time to be on the other side, you will be returned to Earth. However, the experience of visiting the other side puts you in a much better place spiritually on Earth. Your life is transformed for the better.

What Happens to Earthbound Souls?

If a Soul chooses to stay earthbound for any reason, this is not a problem as there is a band of angels who circle the planet and will escort Souls home when they are ready. They sometimes just need an adjustment period from the transition of being physical back to Spirit again. Also individuals, such as myself, have learned how to counsel Souls and convince them that Earth is no longer the place to be without a physical body. No further spiritual growth is possible at that point.

While we have the ability to counsel these Souls, we still need an escort from the other side to take them where they need to go. I work with Jesus/Sananda, Archangel Michael and my Master Guide, Jonathan in assisting earthbound Souls to the other side. Again there is NO benefit for them to stay here. Even though it may comfort you to know they are still around you, it is not good for them. They can help us much more from the Realms of Light.

Comfort from Deceased Loved Ones

Many times our deceased loved ones act as Spirit Guides to comfort and help us cope with their loss. My mother was able to do this for my father upon her death as he was having a hard time dealing with her loss. I think most people are curious as to whether or not there is life after death. My parents had talked about this privately and decided that whoever passed first would try to let the other know if there was life after death. My mother died at age 59 of a massive stroke. She had an inner knowing of how she was going to die and the timing. At one point she mentioned that she would not live to see sixty, and she was not sick at that time. She died on Christmas Eve, one month to the day before she was to turn sixty.

After her passing my father was not able to sleep at night. In order to let him know that she was all right and that she was with him, she appeared, as a silhouette of what she looked like in her younger years, in a ball of Light in the corner of their bedroom. She appeared every night for approximately six months. He said she kept her promise and it comforted him so much. He was extremely disappointed when the ball of Light stopped appearing, but she had brought him to a level where he could move on in his life. My father was a good, hard-working man, but not a spiritual or religious man so I was quite surprised when he shared this experience with me.

My mother was a housewife and mother. She stayed home and raised seven children. That was her purpose. Soon after my youngest brother was out of the "nest," she passed. She ascended to the Light immediately upon passing. Had my father passed first, he would not have been able to comfort her as she comforted him.

Upon my Dad's passing, his Soul had accumulated so much negative energy that he ended up in the Resting Area. The negative energy was a result of stress in his life, which he didn't let go of while on Earth. He was the first Soul I counseled from the Resting Area. Since he was my first and I didn't have any experience or a "How To" book to guide me in knowing how to do this counseling work, I brought him before God on about six occasions before he was finally admitted into the Light.

I eventually came up with a system whereby I would do my counseling work, then check with my Spirit

Guides to see if the Soul was ready and had done their part, before bringing the Soul before God. This made the process much smoother. Now when I bring a Soul before God, they are admitted right away. We are never alone, and this is especially true when we are working with Spirit to help other Souls.

Some Things We Experience Upon Our Return to the Other Side

Upon our return to the other side, our Soul is busy with a greeting, customs clearing, a possible stay in the "Resting Area," and a celebration. After our Life Review, we return to our group, meet with some of our Council Members, and plan our next stage for spiritual growth.

GREETING

Upon the Soul's return they are greeted by their Spirit Guides, Angels, Soul Group Members and deceased loved ones. This process is helpful for Souls who arrive in a confused state. Seeing deceased loved ones helps them to know where they are, and to make their transition easier.

CUSTOM CLEARING

This is where many individuals believe they will meet St. Peter at the Pearly Gates, and he will determine, according to their life accomplishments, whether they will be admitted into Heaven or they have to take the "down" elevator. Fortunately, there is no hell or purgatory or whatever you want to call the place where "bad" people go. The only contraband that is NOT allowed in the higher dimensions is negative energy. Some really "good" people accumulate negative energy as a result of life circumstances. So if you arrive and are weighted down with the negativity you accumulated while on Earth, you are directed to a special location, referred to as the Grey Level, the Basement of Heaven, or the Resting Area. Of those, I prefer the Resting Area. We need to rest after our return, especially if we had a very difficult life.

RESTING AREA

If a Soul had a traumatic/unexpected passing or had a challenging life and did not release the negativity on the Earth plane, then they are escorted to the Resting Area where they recuperate in their own time with the help of Angels and Spirit Guides, and sometimes humans assist from the Earth plane. There is beautiful music and colors that we can't even imagine here on Earth, which help the Souls in their healing process. Hell is a place we create in our mind and we fear that's where we will go. If we clean up our thoughts while on Earth, we can bypass the Resting Area and arrive in the most beautiful place we can't even imagine, which many of us refer to as Heaven.

CELEBRATION

If we pass customs, we go directly to a celebration where Souls welcome us "HOME!" There will be deceased loved ones and individuals we know from this lifetime, as well as other Souls we are familiar with from our group and other lifetimes. If a Soul needs to go to the Resting Area, they will have their celebration afterwards. The more advanced Souls are able to skip the greeting and celebration ceremonies and go straight to their Life Review upon their return if they so desire.

LIFE REVIEW

At this point you are with your Spirit Guides and the Angels that were assigned to you. You compare what you were supposed to accomplish with what you actually accomplished. You are able to see and feel how your thoughts, actions and deeds affected other people. During the Review, if you are not happy with the way you handled any challenges, you are shown different options that you could have chosen and what the outcome would have been.

RETURN TO YOUR GROUP

After the Review, you are escorted to your family/ group of Souls and have an opportunity to get caught up on what's been going on while you were gone.

Council Meeting

Each Soul has a Council of 12 Ascended Masters and one Archangel to oversee their progress. Not all, but some of your Council Members meet with you to ask questions about your recent life. They are interested in the amount of spiritual growth you achieved and if you were able to open your heart and increase your ability to love.

Planning Stage

During the planning stage we meet with our Higher Self, Spirit Guides, Angels and Council Members in putting our future life together. All past lives are revealed so that we can see what has been done and what still needs to be done. We have made a complete cycle at this point and we can stay in the Spirit World and continue to learn or help others, or we can plan our next incarnation. The benefit to incarnating is that the Soul has an opportunity to grow more rapidly as a result of the challenges it has to overcome.

Chapter 6

Some Important Things You Should Know About Death

Over the past twenty years, during both lectures and readings, I have been asked a number of questions about death. There still appears to be a fear factor associated with death. Many who have had Near Death Experiences report that they no longer fear death because they have seen the beauty and peace of the Spirit World.

When I do my spirit releasement work and counsel earthbound Souls, also known as "ghosts," to the Light and if they do not want to go, I explain that their Soul will be returned to Earth after their tour of their new quarters in the Spirit World if they do not want to stay. However, there is no benefit to being on Earth in an energy body. They have an opportunity to be escorted by a Light Being, such as Jesus/Sananda or Archangel Michael to view exactly where they will be. I have only had one Soul who wanted to come back to Earth after his tour of the higher realms. He had issues with his daughter and wanted to clear them up first. Then he promised he would return to the Spirit World, and he did. Because Souls have Free Will they cannot be forced to return to the other side, but they can be coaxed. Once they learn there is nothing to fear, they are happy to return to the Spirit World.

My spiritual guidance has provided the following information regarding our passing from this Earth. This includes answers to questions about fear and pain, peace and anxiety, extending life or early departure, preparing for passing, burial versus cremation, astral traveling, and whether or not we choose death.

What about Fear and Pain?

There is nothing to fear. Our journey to Earth is over and the reward is returning home to where we are loved unconditionally, not only by God, but our fellow souls as well, even those we had issues with while on Earth.

Death does NOT hurt. Once the Soul departs the physical body, even before actual death, the body does not feel pain. The Soul carries the pain vibration. Remember, it is part of our contract to experience pain and suffering. Through the evolutionary/ascension process we are changing this agreement.

Is the Soul Peaceful or Anxious?

The Soul feels peaceful and/or blissful if the passing was of a natural nature. The Soul usually journeys to the higher realms during sleep time prior to death in order to make the transition easier for the Soul. However, if the passing was through unnatural means, such as an accident or murder, the Soul feels confused, scattered, and anxious and might stay earthbound.

Can We Ask to Extend Our Life or Leave Earlier than Planned?

We have the right and the power to ask our Spiritual Council for an extension of life if we so desire.

There are two considerations that will determine whether or not an extension of life is granted:

1. You will continue to grow spiritually.
2. You will assist someone else in their growth process.

On the other hand, the Soul has "Windows of Opportunity" for exit set up in our Life Plan, so if you are feeling you have had enough of life, connect with your Soul and ask if it would be an appropriate time to exit.

Our approximate date, time and place of death are programmed in our DNA. This can be changed if we ask for an extension of life or one of the windows of opportunity opens at the request of the Soul for departure sooner than planned.

If You Are Ready to Prepare for Departure

If you "think" or know that your life is about to come to an end, mentally reach up and place yourself in God's hands and ask for whatever it is that you want at that moment.

Pray/meditate regularly. Keep your connection with God, your Higher Self, your Soul, your Angels and Spirit Guides strong.

Surround yourself with the golden/white Light.

The journey Home will be an easy transition if you don't resist it through the fear vibration.

Burial or Cremation

When I was thinking about whether or not I wanted to be cremated, I thought "no." I was concerned that, if my Soul had not exited the body, being cremated would be like "burning in hell." My guides assured me that the Soul always exits before the body stops functioning so that was not an issue. According to my Spirit Guides, eventually it will be mandatory for the body to be cremated for two reasons: land space requirements and environmental sanitary purposes.

Out of Body or Astral Traveling

While I believed my Spirit Guides when they told me that the Soul carried the pain vibration, I'm one of those people who need proof. When I was suffering so much with the pain of arthritis that some days I couldn't even get out of bed, my Spirit Guides assisted my Soul out of my body to give me some relief. I was semi-conscious of what was going on around me. I could hear my grand-children playing in the next room, but it seemed that I was at quite a distance from them. One thing that was super obvious to me was that I was feeling absolutely no pain in my body. There was my proof.

However, it is not good to go out-of-body too much. When you do "travel," make sure your Angels or Spirit Guides are with you and that Angels are assigned to watch over your physical body while you are absent. Astral "traveling" without spiritual assistance is very dangerous. We are here for the physical experience. While it may feel great to be out-of-body, if the Soul does not return, the individual could slip into a coma state or possibly even die.

As an example, many years ago, a woman came to me for a reading. What she wanted to know was how did her boyfriend die? I felt that the answer to her question should be coming from the doctors — not me. She indicated that there was nothing wrong, physically or medically with him and the doctors and police were baffled as to what caused his death. In checking with my Spirit Guides, they indicated that he was fooling around — pushing and shoving in a playful manner — with some friends, and he was pushed to the floor with such force that his Soul released from the body and he ended up on the other side. Once there he was given a choice to stay or go back. He chose to stay on the other side, so his physical body on Earth had to die.

Our Angels and Spirit Guides can protect us from the so-called "dark" areas. I recently saw the movie *Insidious*, which depicts, on a very dramatic theatrical level, what can happen to a "traveler" who goes too far out without an escort from the Light.

We Do Not Choose Death!

I am not trying to glorify death. I am trying to help you take the fear out of it as there is nothing to fear. I have had people say to me that if death is so great, why aren't we all choosing that path? The answer is that we don't choose death. Our Soul is programmed to exit when the time is appropriate.

When we choose death it is through suicide and in the next section we will discuss why suicide is NOT an option. The important thing to remember is that no matter how difficult life seems, it is our resistance that makes it tough. Release and let go of your struggles and you will notice a big difference.

Chapter 7

WALK-INS, ATTACHMENTS, OVERSHADOWING & EXTRA TERRESTRIALS

I THOUGHT IT WOULD BE APPROPRIATE TO touch briefly on the subjects of Walk-Ins, Attachments, Overshadowing and Extra Terrestrials as they are very common to humanity during this particular lifetime. Not that they did not exist in the past, but a lot is happening on Earth now as a result of the Ascension Process for both Earth and humans.

Walk-Ins

This used to be a rare occurrence, but because of the acceleration of the energy on Earth and the Shifts approaching, Walk-Ins are more common now. Rather than have a physical life end when its mission is done, if the physical body is in good operating condition, a contract is made in the Spirit World for another extension of your twelve Soul parts to exchange positions with you. This arrangement can also be made with others in your Soul Group/Family and even ETs. This saves time from having to go through the birthing process. The Walk-In may be responsible for cleaning up any issues the exiting Soul did not accomplish before exiting.

A Walk-In cannot decide on its own that it wants to occupy your physical body when you are done with your mission or at any time. The contract has to be made with the approval of your Council and Higher Self, and it has to be for the purpose of growth. The Soul extension that has completed its mission will transition to the other side while another part enters the physical body. This transfer usually takes place during a traumatic situation such as an operation or an accident.

Or, depending upon the vibrational level of the two Souls, this transfer can also take place during sleeping hours. There is complete remembrance of what has taken place with the original Soul. One very noticeable difference might be that relationships are not the same. Since the new Soul has not bonded with the relationships of the exiting Soul, and the new Soul has its own agenda, many times relationships end — even real significant relationships such as parents, siblings, spouses, best friends, etc.

Attachments

Attachments are not the same as Walk-Ins. Attachments are earthbound entities or fragments, a small piece of a Soul's energy, looking for a host to be able to continue experiencing life through someone else's physical body. There is no contract here. This is an invasion of your privacy and your Life Plan.

If you are thinking thoughts that are not common or natural for you, or if you are talking out of character and you are not comfortable with what you are saying and wondering "why did I say that," or if you are smoking or drinking when you don't normally smoke or drink, or if you are dressing differently than you normally do, then you may have an attachment to your energy field that is causing these actions.

During meditation, connect with your Spirit Guides and Higher Self, and ask if you are carrying any energy that is not your own. If so, ask that your spiritual guidance assist you in releasing these attachments. If you are not at a point where you are communicating with your Spirit Guides or Higher Self, then seek out the assistance of a Spiritualist or someone who knows how to release attachments. These attachments are not serving your higher good. They are interfering with your Life Plan and spiritual growth, and are developing karma for both of you if they are causing you to do what they want to do. If they are just "nesting" in your energy, they are dragging your energy to a lower vibration. They need to be released and brought to the Light.

Spirit attachment is a very common occurrence. Approximately 70 percent of humanity either has had or will experience an attachment in this lifetime. It is our responsibility to make sure that we release them, even though we didn't invite them to join us or even know that they have attached to our energy.

Attachments can be picked up just about anywhere, but the most common locations are while visiting or working at hospitals, nursing homes, funeral homes and cemeteries, and also during organ transplants. Some of the energy of the organ donor can accompany the organ into your body so be aware of any changes in your thoughts or habits after receiving an organ transplant.

I live near a cemetery and had eight attachments to my energy field when I first learned how to do release-ment work. However, even though I am very diligent in making sure that I am clear of attachments, I seem to attract them regularly. When I notice that I am think-ing negative thoughts or using bad language, I check for attachments and usually find some.

Overshadowing

When I was first exposed to channeling, the person doing the channeling left her body and allowed Spirit to come in and deliver a message to the group. While this was fascinating to me, I decided there was no way I would follow that process. Eventually, I noticed that Spirit was "hovering" over me and working through me from outside of my physical body. The first time I noticed this was when I was at the computer and was typing a meditation to assist individuals with Forgiveness, since I now had expertise on this subject. What I was originally thinking of putting in this meditation would have scared the heck out of people. So Jesus overrode my thoughts and typed a much better version than what I had intended. This is not manipulation, as I had asked Him to be with me and help me with it. I was fascinated and in complete amazement at how I was typing and reading the words as they appeared on the screen.

The words were not coming through my thought process, but through my fingers. Because Jesus' energy was much higher than mine, the reaction I noticed was that my face was very red — worse than being embarrassed or having a hot flash. It was like having a sunburn without the pain. The redness faded shortly after His departure. I had a similar incident while doing a public lecture. There were two gentlemen sitting in the front row who were whispering and pointing at me. It was distracting, but I knew they were talking about my red face, as Jesus was overshadowing me while doing the lecture. I stopped the lecture and explained to everyone why my face was red. I think they thought I was going to explode. After that incident, I studied how I could raise my vibration so that I would not have a reaction to the higher energies that were assisting me. Occasionally, I still get a little red faced, but I think it happens when I have several high level beings with me at one time. It doesn't hurt. Jesus was overshadowed by Melchizedek during His lifetime.

Extra Terrestrials (ETs)

There was a time when I did not believe that ETs existed. Then I switched to thinking that, if they do exist, keep them away from me. I didn't want to deal with them.

I now realize there are many ETs in human form, and I have been guided to assist some of them in "remembering" why they are here. I was doing a reading for a young woman, who wanted specific questions answered. At the end of her reading, Archangel Michael said that he had more information for her. I asked her permission to proceed since Archangel Michael had something he wanted to say to her. She said "No." She had received the information she wanted and didn't have any money to pay for the additional time. I told her that I was willing to provide the information at no cost if she was willing to receive it. She was an ET in human form and was not doing what she came here to do. She was very comfortable with hearing this information from me, as she already had an inner knowing of who she was.

There are many ETs in human form either through the birthing process or as Walk-Ins. They are here to help us as well as raise the vibration of the Planet. I have gained a great deal of respect for them and the sacrifices they have made to incarnate and help us and Mother Earth at this special time in Earth's history.

PART II

SUICIDE IS *NOT* AN OPTION

Chapter 8

WHY SUICIDE IS NOT AN OPTION

WHILE IN PHYSICAL FORM JUST ABOUT ANY-thing we do is accepted as a learning experience and an opportunity to grow to higher spiritual levels — except suicide! Suicide is not acceptable for many reasons.

First of all, we volunteered for the human experience to assist the Source in bringing Light to the Outer World in order to raise the vibration of planet Earth to the point where it will become a mirror effect of the Heavenly Realm. Second, the human body is a very special gift created by God for our use while in physical form and for us to destroy it was never an intention. Third, we have at least three, and possibly five so-called "Windows of Opportunity" planted throughout our Life Plan for escape purposes in case life gets to be more than we can handle.

It is the responsibility of the Soul to exit physical life when the time is appropriate. The Soul is 100% in charge of the decision to end physical life. The Soul will never ask you to do anything to end your life. If you are receiving that type of self-destructive message, it is coming from the negative part of your ego or from an outside negative force and does not have your highest best interest in mind. It is important to override these messages and thoughts by replacing them with positive thoughts of future events or goals you would like to achieve, or by doing something that brings joy into your life, or by any means that is appropriate for you.

Once the Soul reaches the point of knowing its eternal nature and that guidance is available in the higher realms to help during tough times, suicide is not part of the thought process. It is usually experienced by Souls with an abundance of ego energy, who believed they could handle more than they should have included in their Life Plan. During the planning process, before incarnation, a Soul carrying a big ego many times feels that it can accomplish more than it actually can fulfill and dismisses the guidance of its Spiritual Advisors in the Spirit World. This is a mistake, as life in physical form is much different than during the planning stage. Sometimes this overload in the Life Plan leads to overwhelm for the human and thoughts of suicide result as an escape to get away from one's struggles.

God has given Souls Free Will in order to learn through their decisions. If they do not like the outcome of one decision, then they need to change course and make another decision, especially if the new decision will result in their growth. No experience is considered good or bad. It is humanness that places labels of good or bad on their experiences. God perceives mistakes as a teacher and the student/Soul will do much better the next time, as there is no better teacher than the results of a mistake in judgment regarding one's affairs. At some point, it will be necessary for the high-minded Ego Self to let go of control and allow the Soul Self to assist in its decision-making process while on Earth. Also, the Ego Self must learn to allow the higher guidance to help with including lessons in its Life Plan that can be accomplished. As we evolve and enter the Ascension Process, this will happen automatically.

If life becomes too much of a struggle, it is due to resistance on the part of individuals to have things their way. They think they have to solve all of their problems, and when it appears that they are not able to do so, they want to give up. They do not remember that they are a spiritual being first and foremost. They possess very powerful energy to summon assistance from the other side of life. They do not remember that they have a committee to help them along life's path and to help them with life's challenges. So the only thing they can think of doing is to end it all.

Consequences of Suicide

Therefore, God has had to set up restrictions for those who would choose to end their life before it was time for them to depart. The consequences for such an act is that the entire life has to be done all over again, not just the part that they did not complete. For example, if you quit, the ninth grade in school because you do not like the teacher or the lessons are too difficult, or because of health or personal reasons, when you return to school the next year, you do not automatically go on to the tenth grade. You have to repeat the ninth grade over again. It is the same with your Life Plan. If you end life before it is supposed to be completed, when you reincarnate you will have to repeat all the lessons from the life which you ended abruptly. So whatever growth you achieved will be wiped from your Book of Records as not having been accomplished.

You might say "So what!" It might feel worth it to get away from the everyday stress and struggle. But God says "NO!"— It is not worth it. Because if you would only remember to reach up and ask for assistance to help you with these stresses and struggles, your guidance will be there, not to do your lessons for you, but to help you to find a more appropriate way of dealing with the experiences than you have chosen on your own. Our guardians see life as a very simple process, but they are amazed at the different ways humans have found to create the difficulties in our lives. When we return home to the other side after our journey to Earth and do a Life Review, we laugh at how silly we were in our choices.

Seeing Life beyond the Human Concept

As a Soul grows spiritually, as one's spiritual awareness begins to awaken and develop, the Soul begins to see life as its guardians see it. Life is good and life really is simple when we get out of our own way. This was part of the original plan for mankind — to awaken in our own time to who we really are. Not the flesh, blood, bones, muscles, tissues, cells, etc., of the human body, but the part that lives on after the physical body is no longer alive on this Earth.

However, it will take more individuals opening up to who they are — who they really are — for them to see beyond the human concept that because someone has a better education, house, car, and/or more money, these circumstances make them better. This is not so. It is the one who carries the Love energy, the one who carries Compassion and wants to help their fellow human who is the better, even if that individual is homeless and doesn't own a dime. God will allow riches in magnitude proportion to those who will reach up and ask for whatever assistance they need. Nothing is impossible. It is only impossible if you think it cannot happen.

Chapter 9

Traditional & Non-Traditional Causes of Suicide

WHEN I ORIGINALLY RECEIVED INSPIRATION TO begin this book, the information contained in this section on suicide was received first. My spiritual guidance stressed the importance that humans know and understand what is happening during this time of Ascension. The Light (higher vibrating energies) being downloaded to Earth are causing the darkness (lower vibrating energies) to surface. These issues which are surfacing need to be overcome by using the higher vibrating energies of Love, Forgiveness, Compassion, etc. Keep in mind that energy cannot be destroyed. It can only be transformed from positive to negative or negative to positive.

The surfacing of negative energy is not only happening to humans, but to all of God's creations on Earth including our planet as experienced by all the natural disasters that we have been witnessing either personally or via the news.

The Galactic Shift began in 1950. In searching the Internet recently regarding the rate of suicide, I read reports indicating that the suicide rate has been increasing since 1950. It is expected to be at a peak during the two energy shifts of 2012.

I am not a medical practitioner, and definitely not an expert on the subject of suicide; however, I have outlined some things an individual can do to avoid or offset thoughts of suicide. Please ALWAYS consult with a professional who has expertise in this area if you are having even occasional thoughts of ending your life.

Some Traditional Causes of Suicide

* Mental illnesses — chemical imbalance in the brain, depression, schizophrenia, bipolar disorder, etc.
* Being overwhelmed with life's challenges/circumstances.
* Loss of a loved one, job, home, finances.
* Breakup of a relationship.
* Terminal Illness/chronic pain and suffering.
* Physical/verbal/sexual abuse. Bullying of adults and children. Humiliation.

* Alcohol/drug abuse.
* Low self-esteem/disappointment.
* Feeling helpless/hopeless.
* Unresolved trauma.

If you know someone who is going through challenging times, be compassionate and encourage them to seek professional help. As I have already stated, I am not qualified to give advice in this area; however, in addition to professional help, there would also be a benefit to seeking spiritual help. Many times life may seem hopeless when we lose our connection with God, and all the wonderful Light Beings on the other side who are assigned to help us in times of need. They can only help if we ask and allow them to serve us.

Non-Physical Causes

In addition to the traditional causes, there may also be a few non-physical causes:

Entity Attachment. This is when an earthbound spirit attaches to the energy field of another human. If the entity that attaches to a human is strong-willed, it can carry on with life through its host. If the entity committed suicide, there is a very good chance that the host will also have thoughts of suicide.

When I first started to do Spirit Releasement work, a friend of mine said that her daughter was experiencing thoughts of suicide, but she had no desire to die.

She very much wanted to live. We did a session together and discovered that she had two male entities attached to her energy field. One had committed suicide back in the 1800's. He stayed earthbound, which is normal for suicide victims, attached himself to another man and caused him to commit suicide. They joined forces (this piggyback effect made them more powerful) and attached to my friend's daughter who didn't understand what was going on. With the help of Jesus and Archangel Michael, the releasement process was successful and the two attached entities were escorted to the Light.

If your life is good and things are going well, yet you are experiencing thoughts of suicide, first seek a traditional therapist. Also, if you have a strong connection with your spiritual guidance, during meditation or quiet time, ask if you have any energy attached to yours that is not your own. If you have not yet established a connection with your spiritual guidance, or are unable to get a response from your questions, check with a spiritual healer or therapist who knows how to perform releasement work. A word of caution: Be sure to check the references of the person you choose to do spirit releasement work. See if they can provide you with testimonials or contact information for individuals they have worked with regarding spirit releasement. Unfortunately "attachments" are more common that you think.

I plan to write a small eBook on this subject of

Attachment Releasement and will give instructions on how to protect your energy from attachments and how to clear them if you do have any. If you go to my website at www.angelconnections.com and provide your email address, you will be notified when it is available.

Energy Shifts. The download of Light energy to the planet for Ascension purposes is causing havoc with our bodies. This energy has had an effect on different areas of our body through pain and suffering and will have an impact on our nervous system. According to Spirit, this will cause many to consider suicide as a result of the Galactic Shift energy. The important thing to do is seek help immediately. Do whatever you can to offset these thoughts, as they are temporary, but you will need assistance in dealing with them. Some suggestions are listed in the next chapter.

Mission Accomplished. Many evolved Souls are experiencing thoughts that they don't want to be here on Earth anymore. They feel "misplaced" and done with what they came here to do. They want to go "home." While suicide is very rare in this type of situation, it does happen. Just remember who you are. You are here for a specific purpose, and when that purpose is completed, your Soul will exit. Enjoy the "break." Get some rest, and enjoy life, because you will get busy again when the time is Divinely right.

Chapter 10

THINGS WE CAN DO TO AVOID SUICIDE

SUICIDE IS USUALLY APPROACHED BY INDIVIDUALS who are no longer able to cope with life's circumstances. They try drugs, alcohol and other methods of escape, but the problems are still there when morning breaks. When life first starts to appear unbearable:

1. First and foremost consult with a professional therapist — someone qualified to provide assistance with your specific situation.

2. Seek out a friend to talk to — someone who is prone to positive thinking. Someone who looks at life with optimism.

3. Force yourself to look for one small piece of "Light" — something that you can think positive about regarding the difficult situation that is causing you trouble.

4. If it is a relationship issue, know that if it is meant to end, there is nothing you can say or do about it that will make a difference, and suicide is definitely not the answer to any problem. Start thinking about what you can do to make life better for yourself. What steps can you take that will improve your life? What would you be able to do without this person in your life? We are together with individuals for a purpose and when that purpose is completed, it is only natural for the relationship to end and for each individual to move on and have other experiences. Our relationships are programmed in our DNA and there is a time frame connected to them.

5. Reach up and ask your spiritual guides to assist you in correcting any wrongs in the relationship and help you to do whatever is necessary. However, do not manipulate by asking your guides to do something that would be of a controlling nature or to make things happen the way you want them to. While things may "appear" to be hopeless, they are not, as the next door has not opened to you yet, and when it does, it usually is much better than the door that has closed. This is part of life's process. No amount of trying to change destiny is going to make you happy.

6.   Allow life to flow naturally. Happiness happens when you allow the flow of life to unfold as it is meant to be, as it is programmed in your DNA. Don't get caught up in the right or wrong of a situation. Because if it was not meant to happen it would not be happening. Just allow!

7.   Instead of dwelling on what is wrong with your life, think about the things that are RIGHT! Turn whatever appears negative into a positive. Look at your situations from a different angle in order to gain a new perspective on them. Talk your problem out with a trusted friend or loved one. Sometimes others can see things more clearly when they are not directly involved in the situation.

8.   Start busying yourself with helping others who might also be going through rough times. There is nothing more rewarding than reaching out to help another human, especially children, in time of need. Volunteer at a food bank or shelter. Help a shut-in with shopping or errands. Do a kind deed for someone. It helps us to realize that maybe our problems are not as bad as we thought they were.

9.   PRETEND that what is bothering you is NOT bothering you. Develop an attitude that no matter what is going on around you, no matter

what is happening, you are just fine! This may sound silly, but this method has gotten me through many of the tough challenges in life, and it is something I learned from my mother when I was only twelve years old. Human nature is a funny thing. If people know something bothers you, they seem to focus on that whenever they are with you. When I "pretend" that it doesn't bother me, they seem to automatically stop "bugging" me. Maybe they have a contract to help me get over certain issues, but it is very annoying to be annoyed and then have others constantly dwelling upon it. By pretending that certain things don't bother you, this will eventually become your reality.

10. Take control of your thoughts. As soon as you are consciously aware that negative thoughts are flowing through your mind, immediately override them with positive thoughts about the situation, or any situation you can recall from past experiences. Your thoughts create your reality so why not spend your time making sure that what you think is going to create good things in your life! If you dwell on the negative, you will attract more negative situations. You have the power to create the type of life you want through your thoughts. Be positive. Be happy!

11. Remember, the Soul has "Windows of Opportunity" for exit set up in your Life Plan; so if you are feeling that you have had enough of life, connect with your Soul and ask if it would be an appropriate time to exit. The Soul has knowledge that we don't have. There may be a really bright spot ahead for you that you wouldn't want to miss, but you just have to hang in there a little while longer. The Soul always knows what's best. In this situation, you need to be sure that you are connecting with your Soul and not your ego. The ego will tell you what you want to hear. If it is appropriate, the Soul will set up circumstances without your knowledge. When you create the circumstances to take your own life, that is classified as suicide and this is definitely NOT appropriate. The Soul, not the ego part of us, is in charge of how and when we exit physical life.

12. Forgiveness. This is a wonderful tool that God has given us in order to right any perceived wrongs. It is important to not only forgive others for their actions and deeds, but it is equally important to forgive yourself. Don't worry about God, as you will automatically be forgiven by Our Father. If you ask a person for Forgiveness and they refuse by saying that they will never forgive you, don't worry. As long as you are

genuine of heart and are truly sorry for what you have done or said, it does not matter whether or not they forgive you. You are absolved. The burden is on the other person and they will carry it unnecessarily until they decide to let it go.

Forgiveness Test

A simple test to determine if you really have forgiven someone is to think of the situation that caused the problem in the first place. If the negative emotions continue to surface, Forgiveness is not complete. However, when you think of the person or situation that caused you pain and suffering, and a smile comes across your face, know that Forgiveness has truly taken place. In some situations it takes many times of expressing Forgiveness before it actually takes hold. You cannot force Forgiveness to take place. It will happen automatically when the time is right. The important thing is that your desire to forgive or to be forgiven is genuine. And your Soul or Higher Self knows the difference.

Assisting the Younger Generation

I was listening to a teleclass where Dr. Bernie Siegel was the guest speaker. During his talk he mentioned that the suicide rate for ten to fourteen year olds has increased tremendously. And in certain studies of high school teenagers, at least 70% have had thoughts of suicide at some point. This is overwhelming. His advice to these young ones is "eliminate what is bothering you instead of eliminating yourself." That's great advice.

Usually the problems from this age group seem monumental, but this can change overnight. Occasionally a young teenager will accompany a parent to my Angel Workshop. I advise these young ones to connect and work with their Angels, not only with problems, but with their studies, and to be guided to the best path to follow when they have choices placed before them. Teenage years can be difficult (I remember mine), but looking back life wasn't so bad.

Most of the young ones coming to Earth at this time are at a much higher vibration than the rest of us. Their purpose is to assist Earth with the Ascension to a higher dimension. These little ones are coming in at higher vibrational rates than their parents and most of the authority figures in their life. So it must be very frustrating for them to have to deal with us. Our culture expects because they are "kids," they have to do what adults tell them to do for their own good. However, many of these little ones know better than we do what is for their own good. We need to give them a certain amount of leeway in making their own decisions during their early years. They are here to make major changes in all of our earthly systems — education, medical, financial, religion, government — and if we stifle them, they won't be able to do what they came here to do. Treat them with respect. Honor their opinions. Encourage them to be creative. And, most important, love them for who they are, not who you think they should be.

Chapter 11

LESSONS FROM
TWO PAST LIFE SUICIDES

DURING THIS LIFETIME I AM BALANCING TWO past lives where I had committed suicide. In each case, I believed my actions would not be detected or classified as suicide, but we can't fool our Keepers of the Records of Truth. I believe that writing this book and particularly this section on suicide is part of my contract to help humanity know that under NO circumstances is it acceptable to take one's own life.

A Rejected Wife

Back in the 1600's in a remote farmland area in France, my father had much acreage to take care of and only daughters to help out. It was his hope that his six daughters would marry and their husbands would take up residence on the farm to assist with the many responsibilities. Since I was the eldest daughter, I was the first to marry. It was wonderful at first, but after a few years things worked in a very negative pattern for me. I was not able to get pregnant, which in those days was the major responsibility of the women — to bear children. My husband co-habituated with one of my younger sisters and she became pregnant. I was broken-hearted and thought that by telling my father about the betrayal, he would banish my husband from the premises. Much to my surprise, my father was elated at the fact that there would be an offspring and maybe, just maybe, it would be a boy who would be able to take over the responsibilities of the farm later on. I felt betrayed by my father as well and decided I no longer wanted to live. I could not bear being a part of the joyous event of my sister giving birth to my husband's child. I was not strong enough to be able to live under the circumstances which had turned my life upside down. Since one of my responsibilities was to cook the meals for everyone, I secretly stopped eating knowing that I would die and that was fine with me. I just wanted to get away from the intense pain I was feeling in my heart. It was too much for me to bear. I don't know how long it took, but I finally passed before the baby was born. My sister and my husband eventually married in that lifetime and had five more children, four of which were boys, and that made my father very happy.

When I reached the Life Review stage upon my

return to the other side, it was shown to me that it was a common occurrence for families to intermingle for the purpose of reproduction — to keep the family line going. It was the mindset at the time that you put up with whatever was necessary, whether it was acceptable or unacceptable, and lived with it. Unfortunately I looked at it from the negative perspective and chose to opt out. This is one of the lifetimes I am balancing in this lifetime, and it is amazing to know the pieces of the puzzle that have fit together. I was able to recognize the past in the present. I want to thank the characters in this lifetime who have assisted me in my spiritual growth by helping me to get it right this time.

Kidnapped for Trade Secrets

In the 1700's in England (I was a male in that lifetime), I was a bookkeeper for a very wealthy business owner. Other businessmen envied him and wanted to know his secret of success. Since they were not able to get any information from him directly, they kidnapped me and kept me in a dungeon-type place. The tool they used to try and get me to talk was food. Every day at mid-morning and mid-afternoon, they would bring a wonderful array of delicious looking and smelling foods — foods fit for a king. They knew my one weakness and that weakness was food. Unfortunately, the only way I would have been able to partake in these feasts was to reveal my employer's secrets to his success. One of my strong points in that lifetime was loyalty. The first few days were torture. After not eating or drinking anything for a while, the food had an opposite effect on me. The smell made me sick to my stomach. At that point I wanted to reveal the secrets in order for them to take the food away.

Once again, in that lifetime, I died of starvation. Spirit classified this as a suicide as it was my Free Will decision not to eat. I knew that I would eventually die without food. In my Life Review it was shown that, in this difficult circumstance, I could have provided them with false information as if these were the real "secrets" so they would release me. That would have given me the time necessary to set up protection so that they would not be able to kidnap me again. These men were not murderers, they were greedy. Their only intention was to obtain information that they could use to become wealthy. My reaction carried it to the extreme, and I am working out the results in this lifetime.

Strangely enough, an issue I have brought forward to experience in this lifetime is over-eating. I will definitely overcome this before the end of this lifetime. It's all about balance.

Small Deeds Save Lives
Many years ago I attended a seminar at the Edgar

Cayce Institute in Virginia Beach. Dr. Raymond Moody was talking about one of the patients he interviewed when he was doing research on Near Death Experiences. He indicated that this woman reached the Life Review stage during her short journey to the other side. In her review, she saw herself walking down a busy street while another woman walked toward her from the opposite direction. As they passed each other the patient smiled at the other woman. The patient did not remember this event from her earthly life and didn't know why she smiled. However, it was noted that she grew spiritually as a result of that small deed. The other woman was heading home to her apartment to commit suicide. When she received the smile, something inside of her "clicked" and she decided not to commit suicide, but to continue on with life. Saving the life of another human always results in tremendous spiritual growth.

Always Work with Spirit

No matter how "tough" life seems to be, know that within a moment of time things can change, as it did in the above case. This is why it is so important to make the connection with Spirit (your Soul, Higher Self, Spirit Guides, Ascended Masters, Angels and/or God.) When circumstances seem unbearable, to the point where you want to escape, just reach up through your thoughts or prayers and ask for HELP. Spirit works through others to help us get to where we need to be and to stay on our path and complete our mission. It's why we came here to begin with.

Chapter 12

EUTHANASIA

THERE IS A MIXED BELIEF ON THE SUBJECT of euthanasia. While it seems humane to be released from the pain and suffering, especially if someone has a terminal illness, according to spiritual laws euthanasia is still classified as suicide. The only time it would not be considered a suicide is if a medical professional or loved one took matters into their own hands, without the knowledge of the terminally ill individual, and assisted in their passing sooner rather than when the Soul determined it was time to depart. However, when a terminally ill individual asks for assistance in ending their life, in the higher realms this is classified as a suicide, because they are consciously requesting assistance.

Methods Beyond Pain

Since the human race chose pain and suffering as a

means of growing spiritually, why opt out while in the suffering mode? Growth is taking place and anything that has been accomplished up to that point would be erased, and another lifetime would have to be scheduled to do it all over again. Staying here on Earth and completing your Life Mission would be a much better decision.

There are things you can do to ease your symptoms, in addition to what your medical caretaker prescribes. One method is out-of-body. When the Soul is not in the physical body, pain does not exist. I know this from firsthand experience. When I was suffering so terribly with rheumatoid arthritis symptoms and could hardly move or get out of bed, my Angels would assist my soul out of the body to give me some relief. For relief of pain, out-of-body does not mean astral traveling. The Soul can hover above you in the same room. Always make sure your Angels and/or Spirit Guides are with you if you choose to go out-of-body.

Another method is to connect with your Higher Self, Spirit Guides and/or Angels and ask them to help you deal with whatever you need. When I had a function I needed to attend, but was not sure I would be able to go, I would ask my Angels to be with me and help me to do whatever was necessary. The Angels would run their energy through mine and it gave me the strength I needed to get through the day or event. Anytime is a good time to "ask," however, just before falling asleep at night is an excellent time to put in any requests you may have as sometimes we get the answers in our dreams.

Importance of the Message

Sananda had been stressing through me for many years the importance of the message "suicide is not an option." One Sunday while speaking at a church service, I only intended to say "suicide is not an option." Instead I went on and on and on regarding Spirit's concern about the rate of suicide at all ages. This sometimes happens when you allow Spirit to speak through you. When I consciously became aware that I was carrying the point far too long, I interjected with the comment, "You would think I was suicidal by the way I'm carrying on," and it lightened up the intensity of the energy.

While I believed that what Sananda was telling me was truth, it is a common belief today that euthanasia is acceptable if a person has a terminal illness and is going to die anyway — that God would not want them to suffer. This, too, seemed logical, so I asked Sananda, once again, if there were any circumstances when suicide would be acceptable. The answer was an absolute "NO!" His explanation was that humans decided upon pain and suffering as a means of spiritual growth, therefore, there would be no benefit to ending one's life because they were in pain and suffering. The Soul will exit when it is Divine Time.

The Coming Energy Shifts

The reason Sananda and other wonderful Light Beings are stressing this message is because of the effects the energy shifts are going to have on humanity. It has been happening on an increasing level since 1950 when the Galactic Shift began. As I have already mentioned, the energy being downloaded to Earth has been a catalyst in helping the negativity to surface and to be transmuted into positive energy. We have felt the effects in our physical bodies through various ailments and illnesses, such as fibromyalgia, arthritis, headaches and chronic fatigue. These energies will also have an effect on our nervous systems, which will cause some to experience thoughts of suicide. I am not sure exactly how the energies will affect the nervous system, but statistics show that the rate of suicide is increasing. This is a heads-up for us to take whatever steps are necessary to offset these thoughts. Overriding negative thoughts with pleasant thoughts, filling our day with enjoyable events, and surrounding ourselves with optimistic people will help tremendously.

Chapter 13

DID ELVIS COMMIT SUICIDE?

DID ELVIS COMMIT SUICIDE? SEVERAL YEARS ago my spiritual guidance informed me that Elvis Presley's death was recorded in his Life Book of Records as a suicide. It was not an accidental overdose — it was intentional. According to my guides, he deliberately took additional amounts of his medicine knowing what the outcome would be.

No matter how we try to camouflage our intentions, our spiritual overseers know our thoughts and the truth of any situation, and that is what is recorded in the Akashic Records. Always remember that your thoughts create your reality and that is why it is so important to think positive, uplifting thoughts.

A Channeled Message from Elvis
While working on this section, my spiritual guid-

ance said that they would bring Elvis to me so that he could provide a message to humanity regarding his death. By doing so, this would assist him in his spiritual growth and possibly help someone on Earth now who might be contemplating suicide. Following is the message I received from Elvis for all of his wonderful fans:

I ask God to bless each and every one of you. I am very grateful for those of you who supported and accepted me for who I was. I love you all, and I have come forward through this medium to express my regrets for ending my life as I did. There was too much stress. The whole world seemed to come crashing in on me and I didn't know how to handle it. I led a very sheltered life. I am not complaining as I see that the ones who were overseeing my career progress had my highest best interests in mind. If they had not sheltered me in that way I would have ended my life much sooner than I did.

The reason I want to share my experience with all of you is to let you know that suicide is not the way to go. The reason we have physical lifetimes is for the purpose of growing spiritually. I messed up, and I have no one to blame but myself. I was a spiritual person. I loved spiritual music. It made me feel good inside. It made me feel closer to God. Then I went into Rock and Roll. While this was not bad, I loved that music as well, but it put me on a different path. I was not happy with the tight schedule they booked for me. I didn't have time to pursue the things I loved to do in life. Even when I got married our lives were not private, and I so wanted to have privacy. Looking at my life from this side, I wish I had done many things differently, but it is too late now to worry about that. I will do much better the next time out. Priscilla and I will have another opportunity to experience love in another life. I am sorry to say that I was not a good mate to her. I neglected her needs. Life was all about me and my schedule and doing what others wanted me to do. I should have put my foot down and said "NO! I am retiring and from this point forward I am going to do what I want to do." In my Life Review, I saw that this would have been the best thing for all of us.

I see that I made a very big mistake by "checking out" too early. And I am sharing this with you so that if you are thinking of doing as I did, my advice is DON'T! Get help. Talk with someone. It is amazing how quickly things can change when you deal with your problems instead of giving in to them.

I am looking forward to seeing many of you again in my next lifetime. You will not recognize me as I am planning on being a Preacher who will add to the ministry through spiritual song. I will not have a single church where I am the minister. The world will be my church. I will travel, preach the word of God and then follow that with a concert of spiritual music and song. The audience will participate in song, not just listen. I see that I will be able to be successful, have a wonderful life and help many more individuals through the word of God and spiritual song. See you in the future.

~Elvis

After Elvis Presley's energy left, I asked my Spirit Guides if they could share any additional information regarding Elvis' return to Earth. I was told that, at this time, the plan is that he would be born in the year 2015 and would become a Preacher in the year 2039. He will be a male, reside in the U.S., but will travel the world. More specific details were not revealed to me at that time.

A Reminder about Being Happy and on One's Spiritual Path

One thing I would like to reiterate regarding whether or not you are following your spiritual path: if you are happy with life and what you are doing, you are on your path. If you are not happy, then you need to make changes. Elvis was not happy as he was not following his path. He allowed others to control his every move, which stripped him of his Free Will. While the intention of these individuals was good, that does not matter. His highest good was not being served. We looked at Elvis as successful in just about every aspect of life — fame, fortune, success, looks. It appeared that he had it all. It was surprising to learn that he had slipped off his path. How could anyone be that successful and not be doing what he was supposed to be doing? The key is that he was not happy. When you are happy with what you are doing, then you are doing the right thing for you. It's your life. Don't live it to please others. Live it to please yourself.

Anger and the Spiritual Path

It is only natural for us to get angry from time to time. It is not something we consciously plan to do. It is an emotion that is triggered by situations when we feel abused, taken advantage of, treated unfairly, wronged or feel powerless. This is how Elvis felt in his life, powerless to make the decisions to do what he wanted to do, things that would make him happy. He is now able to see the error of his ways, but it is too late. Don't allow anyone to take away your power to follow your path no matter how great their intentions may be.

Momentary anger is a healthy expression of emotion. However, when we hold onto it and don't allow it to be released, it becomes toxic to our mind, body and spirit. Forgiveness is the antidote for anger — for self and others. In time, you will be able to view the situation that caused you to be angry as a comedy and will be able to laugh at how you reacted. This is when true Forgiveness is realized.

Stress and the Spiritual Path

"Stress" is a word coined by Dr. Hans Selye in the 1930's to describe the "rate of wear and tear on the body." Stress is known to cause and/or aggravate illnesses such as heart disease, cancer, arthritis, diabetes, ulcers, asthma, hyperthyroidism, as well as headaches, neck/backaches, dizziness, fatigue, anxiety and a variety of other ailments. It is important that we learn how to manage and control the many sources of daily stress around us. We can do this in two ways:

1. Change whatever can be changed in our physical environment.
2. Change our thinking or attitude towards the things we cannot change.

Keep in mind that our thoughts create our reality. You are the only one who can control what you are thinking. The more you "switch" your negative thoughts into positive thoughts, the better life will be. An important thing to keep in mind is that it is NOT the people or situations in our life that cause our stress. It is our REACTION to them that cause DIS-EASE in our life and eventually in our bodies through illness. Or the worst scenario would be the ultimate reaction of committing suicide, as Elvis confessed to, as a result of not being able to cope with his circumstances. He admitted that, it was not the people around him making decisions for him, it was his inability to do what he wanted.

When we find ourselves in stressful situations, the "fight or flight" mechanism is triggered and certain physiological changes occur in the body such as increased heart rate and blood pressure and our muscles tighten. This was necessary at the early stages of evolution for survival purposes. But we don't have a way of shutting it off. It is automatic and gives us superhuman powers during emergency situations.

For instance, many years ago, my husband was working on an old 1959 Chevy Impala in the backyard of my mother's house. He had jacked up the front end, put a chaise lounge cushion on a dolly and rolled himself under the car. The jack snapped, the car fell on him and because of the height of the dolly and cushion, the car pinned him down so he couldn't roll out from under it. The car was very heavy on his chest. Luckily for him my mother happened to pass by as the jack snapped. She immediately realized the danger and single-handedly picked the car up long enough for him to be able to get out from under it.

It was the stress of the moment that gave her the super strength to be able to lift the car up. Later when the emergency was over and everyone was amazed that she was able to lift the car and hold it up long enough for him to get free, she tried to do it again and it was not possible. She couldn't get it to budge even a fraction of an inch. She didn't think. She did what she could in the moment of need.

A good antidote for stress is deep breathing. When you feel yourself losing control as a result of being exposed to stressful situations, whether at work, home, school or even the sports arena, take the time to do some deep breathing and you will feel your body relax immediately.

Trauma and Suicide

Many people have grown up in very harsh situations and have endured serious trauma that often causes them to consider suicide. We cannot judge the Life Plans of other people, we can only offer them our support when we are able, and we can also not "make them bad" by saying, "They must have done something bad in a past life." It is possible that they were a great saint in a past life and are here with us enduring difficult times for reasons beyond our understanding to assist us in raising the vibration of our planet. It is important for these individuals, whether or not they were saints in a previous lifetime, to change their thoughts about their difficult experiences. When they begin to see their oppressors as their greatest teachers, they will see a rise in their spiritual vibration. For some people, changing thoughts happens quickly, for others it is over time. Once they are able to resolve their anger, accept and forgive and change their thoughts surrounding a certain situation, they will be working through their life lessons for the benefit of us all.

Chapter 14

ASK AND YOU SHALL RECEIVE — HOW I BATTLED DEPRESSION AND WON!

I GREW UP THE THIRD CHILD IN A FAMILY OF seven children. I guess we were poor, but I didn't seem to think too much about that as everyone I knew was experiencing similar circumstances. It wasn't until I got out on my own, started earning my own income and could buy and do whatever I wanted, that I realized that I had grown up during difficult economic times.

Perhaps the reason this didn't matter to me was, while we didn't have a lot of material things, we had love. Not the kind of love that was expressed in words, but the kind of love that was unspoken through actions and deeds. The protection of our parents and the support from our brothers and sisters, especially when someone from outside the family tried to step in and harm or criticize one of us, caused a warm feeling of safety.

Asking for What You Need

While the comforts of the material world and what money can buy are great, what is even greater is when you don't have the money, you do have the ability to reach up to your spiritual guidance and ask for what you want and need. This is the power of the God within working with the God above to bring peace, joy, love, happiness, abundance and all good things into your life. This is a God-given right all humans possess, but many do not understand the concept of "Ask and You Shall Receive." You need to let go of the negative, desperate emotions and trust, believe, and know that you will be given what you really need, and it will find its way to you in Divine Time. Also, do not try to give your Spirit Guides, Angels, and/or God specific instructions on how to bring you what you want and need. They have their own ways and means of serving you, so you only interfere when you try to dictate "how" they should do their work.

Asking for Money

Let me explain what I mean. I have a friend who was struggling financially. She was two months behind in all of her payments. She kept asking her spiritual guidance for help in a specific way. She wanted to work to earn the money and was putting restraints and restrictions on her request by telling them how she wanted the money to come to her. When she let go and allowed Spirit to bring her what she needed, she got more than she needed. Her hot water heater broke and caused some water damage in her home. At first she was devastated as it "appeared" that she would be deeper in debt as a result of having to replace the hot water heater, carpet, and some personal belongings. She wasn't thinking clearly. However, she was reminded that she had homeowners insurance. The insurance settlement not only covered the replacement of the hot water heater, but she had enough to bring her bills up to date, as she chose not to replace some of the personal items that were lost.

There is a certain satisfaction in working and earning the money to buy what you want. But if things get to the point where more is going out than you have coming in, you must have an alternative source to assist in making ends meet or cut back on expenses. I don't mean to disillusion you about the ease of asking and receiving, but it has worked for me and many others, so why not try it and see what happens for you.

The "Secret" to Asking

The ability to ask and receive is a gift from God. He wants all of us to prosper. The "Secret" that many do not know about is that once your spiritual vibration comes within the range of the 5th dimension, Ascended Master level, twenty-four hours each day and seven days a week, your manifesting what you want and healing your physical body happen automatically. You are in your true God state at that level of vibration.

Individuals such as Sai Baba, who are vibrating spiritually at even higher levels, have the ability to manifest what they are asking for by holding out their hand and receiving their request. Usually this is done on behalf of others to demonstrate that this is an ability given to mankind when the time is appropriate. To give that type of gift to someone vibrating at the 3rd dimensional level would be a misuse of God's gift as they would not be spiritually mature enough to use it for the highest best of all.

The gift of automatic healing and manifesting one's heart desires is something that is earned as a result of spiritual growth and bestowed upon the individual when the time is Divinely right, not just because an individual feels that they are at a point where they have earned the right. We have quite an array of non-physical individuals looking out for us and keeping track of our growth, and they know better than we do when we are ready.

ABUSING THE GIFT

If a person earns this right and abuses the power,

they will find that their ability diminishes. It is not a case of you earn this power and possess it for the balance of your earthly life. If you earn it and abuse it, it will be taken away until sometime later when you have matured enough to realize it is not Aladdin's Lamp, and you can have more than your fair share just for the asking. There is a right way and a wrong way to use this powerful gift so be careful when you find that you have the ability. Use it for your highest good and for the highest good of others as well.

When We Don't Receive What We Ask For

Many times we ask for things and wait and wait for them to arrive. When they don't show up, we feel that we don't deserve them or God doesn't want us to have them. The truth is that we set up unconscious, invisible blocks through our thought processes and this is what prevents our desires from manifesting. Another reason why things may not come to us for the asking is that our spiritual guidance may be able to see that it would cause more harm than good in our life, and they hold back on the request because a lesson is not attached to it. Our spiritual guidance cannot interfere with the lessons we have placed in our Life Plan.

This is part of the plan for humanity and specific individuals have come to Earth from time to time to demonstrate these qualities for us. Jesus was one such individual who came to show us the way, but we were not ready to see, at that time, that we are Gods-in-training.

How I "Battled" Depression and Won!

When my marriage ended, I fell into a temporary state of deep depression. Nothing like I had ever experienced before. I knew I was "sinking" emotionally, but I didn't seem to care. It's strange, but there seemed to be a comfort level wallowing in my own misery. I didn't answer the door. With Caller ID, I only talked with certain select individuals. I didn't want to get out of bed. Had to force myself to shower and get out of my night clothes. I didn't go anywhere unless it was absolutely necessary. After three months of being in this state, I realized that that was NOT where I wanted to be. It no longer felt comfortable. Because of my connection with Spirit, and specifically Jesus, I reached up and asked Him to help me get out of the dark hole I had dug for myself. I realized I was at a point of needing help to get back on track.

One night I was attempting to meditate and because my vibration was so low, I didn't feel as though I had made a connection so I mentally called out to Jesus once again to help me. Instantly, I felt the presence of a "huge" being standing right in front of me. My Living Room has an eight foot ceiling and this being was definitely touching the ceiling. It was Jesus. He was answering my call for help. I sensed that He was reaching His hand out (palm up) for me to take. Much to my surprise, instead of reaching out to take His hand, I pulled away and thought I was going to go through the back of my marshmallow cushiony meditation chair. I started to cry and said, "Jesus, please don't go until you get me out of this dark hole I am in. I don't know why I am acting this way, but please HELP ME!"

Suddenly, my body bolted forward in the chair and my nose almost touched the carpeting. When I pulled myself upright, He was gone and miraculously my depression was gone as well. I couldn't believe it. I felt good all over. I was happy and had a perpetual smile on my face. I just kept saying "THANK YOU, THANK YOU, THANK YOU," as I was so grateful to be free of the negativity. The depression symptoms have not returned. The experience of depression created within me a great deal of compassion for those who live with that condition on a regular basis.

Again, the reason I am sharing this personal experience is to let you know that you have the same ability and the right to ask Spirit for help as I did. Spirit does not discriminate. We are all God's children, but we have to ASK for help. It is not automatic because God should know what our needs are. Our Free Will dictates that, if we want help, we have to ask for it. So again, I reiterate "Ask and You Shall Receive" if you are struggling with life and its many challenges.

PART III

ASCENSION AND BECOMING AN ASCENDED MASTER

Chapter 15

WHAT IS ASCENSION?

IT IS THE PURPOSE OF ALL SOULS TO REACH THE Ascended Master level of vibration at the 5th Dimension before they have completed their mission on Earth no matter how many lifetimes it takes. Most Souls have had hundreds and possibly thousands of lifetimes. Until now, only a few hundred humans have achieved this mission. At this specific time in Earth's history, multi-millions of Souls will reach the Ascended Master level of vibration, because of the two energy shifts taking place — Planetary Alignment, which is a three day process, and the Galactic Shift, which takes approximately 150 years — and because of the recent change in requirements for the Ascension Process.

Ascension Is Many Things

Ascension is actually many things. Some of these include transitioning our energy vibration from 3rd to 4th to 5th Dimensions, transforming a carbon-based body to a crystalline Light Body, the process of dying while still alive, and the Ego and Soul merging with the Higher Self as one Light Being. Ascension is also acceleration of spiritual consciousness, being freed from the cycles of Karma and reincarnation, and the integration of male and female energies. Explanations are included below.

Transition of Our Energy Vibration
from 3rd to 4th to 5th Dimension Levels

Each Dimension contains many different levels of vibration. I am not sure exactly how many levels there are for each Dimension, I believe there are twelve, but any growth we attain by working through our life lessons brings us to a higher level within the Dimensional vibration we are currently occupying. To get from the 3rd Dimension to the 5th Dimension vibration takes many hundreds, possibly thousands, of lifetimes as we grow at our own rate through our Free Will decisions.

Transition of Our Carbon-Based Body
to a Crystalline Light Body

Each and every carbon-based cell in our human body will physically explode. This explosion causes inflammation, and the inflammation causes pain. The old carbon-based cells will be replaced as crystalline or Light cells — Light meaning spiritual energy. We will be creating Light or Spiritual bodies that will serve us better as we rise into the higher dimensions. This is why self-healing will occur more easily and quickly once we reach the Ascended Master vibration. If we are scheduled to go through the Ascension Process in this lifetime, it will be programmed in our Life Plan blueprint contained in our DNA and will be triggered automatically when the time is Divinely right. We do not have any control over the activation of this process. It is orchestrated by our growth here on Earth. We can take steps to consciously accelerate our growth. However, once the Process is triggered, there is no turning back. Since we have trillions of cells in our body, it is not possible for all of them to explode at the same time. That would literally kill us. The Process happens over many years. Remember, the higher our vibration, the less pain and suffering we will experience.

The Process of Dying While Still Alive

This has to do with the cellular transformation. In the past, the transformation of the physical body to a Light body happened after physical death. Now we are experiencing the transformation while still in physical form.

The Personality (Ego)/Soul/Spirit (Higher Self) Merge into One Light Being

While vibrating at the 3rd Dimension level, we are experiencing life through our ego/personality self. Eventually, as we grow spiritually, the ego/personality self connects with the Soul Self. This is the most difficult transition to make as the ego self has been in charge for many lifetimes and doesn't want to give up "control" to the Soul. However this is a necessary process in the Path to Ascension. Once the Ego and Soul connect and work together, our vibration is at the beginning of the 4th Dimension. Finally, as we enter the beginning level of the 5th Dimension, the Ego Self and Soul Self, working in tandem, connect with the Higher Self, the Spirit part of us on the other side, and allow the Higher Self to guide us along our spiritual path.

Acceleration of Spiritual Consciousness

The acceleration of the higher level energy being downloaded to Earth is also causing spiritual awakening at an accelerated rate. Individuals begin to realize that they are spiritual beings and have a craving to reach the highest level possible in this lifetime. They realize they have a purpose and are anxious to know what that purpose is and then to do what they came here to do.

BEING FREED FROM THE CYCLES OF KARMA AND REINCARNATION

When we reach the Ascended Master vibration, we no longer have to deal with karmic issues. We do not have to reincarnate either unless we choose to do so. If we decide to reincarnate, we will still have to work through lessons, while helping others to achieve the 5th Dimension vibration.

INTEGRATION OF MALE AND FEMALE ENERGIES

Have you noticed that the male and female roles have changed, especially during this lifetime? We now have equal opportunities and pay for both men and women. We have stay at home dads, taking on the traditional female role. And we have women joining the armed forces and fighting wars taking on a traditional male role. This is part of the integration process. We are no longer divided and classified that because we are a woman or a man we can only do certain jobs or tasks. On the other side, we are energy beings — not male or female. As humans we need both genders for reproduction purposes.

Different Types of Ascension

At this time in Earth's history, there are two types of Ascension for humanity — Spiritual and Physical. Planet Earth is also ascending at the same time and this is referred to as Planetary Ascension.

SPIRITUAL ASCENSION

Opening awareness of who we are spiritually. We have experienced this process in many other lifetimes. However, when we return to physical form in a new lifetime, we have forgotten who we are and have to open our awareness again. Fortunately, the two energy shifts of 2012 will provide humanity with an even greater opportunity to finally recognize that we are "God" Beings and have so much more potential than we can possibly believe.

PHYSICAL ASCENSION

This process can be very painful as each and every cell in our body transforms from carbon-based to crystalline Light Body. This transformation process involves the physical explosion of each and every cell in our body. The explosion causes inflammation and the inflammation creates the painful effect, such as experienced with Fibromyalgia and most autoimmune conditions. Since we have trillions of cells in our body, this process happens gradually over many years and not all at the same time.

PLANETARY ASCENSION

In addition to humanity's Ascension, our planet Earth is also ascending, rising from 3rd to 4th Dimensions then on to the 5th Dimension. As occupants of Earth we are assisting in the planet's ascension process through raising our own vibration. We are partners with Planet Earth in our journey to Ascension. Earth is a God created entity and we are working together to rise to higher vibrational levels. Therefore, we are experiencing Planetary Ascension along with Mother Earth. As we raise our vibrational level we will be able to go through the Earth's changes with the greatest amount of ease.

According to Dr. Joshua David Stone's material, when we are finished with Planetary Ascension, we will still have to go through: Solar, Galactic, Universal, Multi-Universal and Cosmic Ascension in order to return "home" to the Godhead. We can work on the other levels of Ascension at the same time we are working on Planetary Ascension. However, it will be much easier to get through the other levels once we have completed Planetary Ascension.

Ascension Requirements Revised

Originally life on Earth started in Spirit form — no physical body. Ascension was happening very quickly as there were no challenges, no duality, no karma to deal with. Souls were able to return "Home" basically at the same level they entered Earth. Therefore no real growth was taking place. When the physical body was created, new rules for Ascension were put in place making it more difficult to achieve spiritual growth. These rules were so difficult that it was almost impossible to reach the Ascension level. The physical body, the "amnesia" effect, and ultimate karma caused the difficulty. When the majority of humanity was not making progress, it appeared that the experiment, creating heaven on Earth, was going to fail. It was time for another revision. Therefore, God went to Source and requested that the requirements be relaxed so that more humans could reach the level they were destined to reach. Source agreed.

It was decided that we would no longer have to go through the Ascension Process on an individual basis. It was time for more humans to reach the higher vibrations and that could be accomplished in group or mass form. Therefore, according to my spirit guides, in 1950 at the start of the Galactic Shift, God initiated the revision to the requirements for Ascension, which will allow multi-millions of humans to reach the Ascension level of vibration in the very near future.

ORIGINAL ASCENSION REQUIREMENTS

The original requirements for individual Ascension required that we breakthrough the veil between the physical and spirit worlds, dissolve 100% of our Karma, and reunite all Soul fragments.

BREAKING THROUGH THE VEIL

For most individuals meditation has been the key to breaking through the veil between the two worlds. Meditation helps us to connect with our Spiritual Team on the other side, whose responsibility it is to assist us along our spiritual path. Because of the density of our low vibrating energy, this was a very difficult task to accomplish. Therefore, many humans were stuck in the mindset that they were "human" only. Not being able to make the connection with their Spiritual Team for assistance, many believed, and some still do, that we are living in hell while on Earth.

DISSOLVE 100% OF KARMA

Karma came about as a result of witnessing, in our Life Review, how we hurt others, and we wanted to correct or balance those acts by scheduling the same or similar experiences for ourselves as a tool to grow to higher spiritual levels. Unfortunately, it ended up becoming a vicious cycle of repeating the same acts over and over again and not actually resolving them. Under the original rules for Ascension each person was responsible for dissolving all of their Karma. This was extremely difficult for humans and why the requirements had to be revised.

Reunite All Soul Fragments

Many times when we experience trauma or stressful situations (such as abuse), fragments of our Soul may exit and remain in limbo here on Earth. It is our responsibility to bring those parts back and reunite them with the Soul in the physical body. If these parts are unwilling to rejoin the Soul, they need to be directed to the Light to reunite with the Parent Soul on the other side. We can call upon our Spirit Guides and Angels to escort any part of the Soul, which has disconnected from the physical body, to the Parent Soul on the other side. This was very difficult because most humans were not aware of this responsibility while in physical form. Occasionally, by "coincidence" Soul fragments would reunite, but it was not through conscious effort. Again, it was necessary to revise this rule as most humans were not aware that they needed to do anything.

Ascended Souls

During the time of individual Ascension, a span of approximately 10 million years, only a few hundred souls achieved the Ascension level. This was due to our being stuck in the 3rd Dimension vibration as human beings and not remembering that we are spiritual beings and why we were here on Earth.

According to my spiritual guidance, President John F. Kennedy and Walt Disney were the last two humans to reach the Ascended Master level as individuals before the requirements changed. They had met all the original requirements, which were very difficult to accomplish.

NEW REVISED GROUP ASCENSION REQUIREMENTS

Again, because the requirements for Ascension were so difficult to achieve, God handed down revised requirements to be accomplished in mass or group form. We must still open our awareness to whom we are spiritually and now it is easier to break through the veil. Instead of dissolving 100% of our Karma, we only have to dissolve 51%, and we only need to reunite as many Soul fragments as possible, but not all fragments. This is truly a blessing for humanity.

It is expected that through Mass/Group Ascension, multi-millions of individuals will be able to reach the level of Ascension by 2040. While this may not be the majority of humanity, it is a huge number compared with the few hundred who reached the Ascension level under the old requirements. Ascension doesn't stop with the 2012 energy shifts. It will continue until each and every human ascends, no matter how long or how many lifetimes it takes.

AWAKENING TO OUR SPIRITUAL NATURE

Due to the acceleration of the energy on the planet, the veil is very thin now, and it is much easier to access the unseen world and establish a connection with our

Spiritual Team. Also, the Angelic Realm has been doing everything possible to connect with us and help us with our "Awakening" Process.

An important part of the Ascension Process is for the Ego to unite and work in tandem with the Soul. The Soul is that spark of Divine Light which exists in the physical body. The Ego part of us does not have to dissolve or go away completely; it just needs to calm down and allow the Soul to direct our path. This is very difficult and takes quite some time as the Ego has directed our lives for multi-millions of years. However, once the Ego steps out of the way, our fears subside and the Awakening Process begins.

The next step of the Ascension Process is for the Soul and Ego combined to connect with the Higher Self, the spiritual part of us that resides on the other side. When we allow our Higher Self to provide guidance to us here on Earth, we are in the Ascended Master vibration. And life is good and so much easier, because we know that what we are doing is right for us even if everyone around us is telling us "NO!"

Dissolve Only 51% of Our Karma

The Lords of Karma, a group of highly evolved Light Beings, were recently assigned by God to help humanity rid ourselves of unnecessary Karma. Unnecessary Karma is the holding on of old issues that have been resolved.

Apparently, we have been hanging onto these old issues as if they were a "treasure." In order to raise our vibrational level of energy, it is now absolutely necessary for us to let go of what we do not need, and these special beings of Light are willing to help us if we call upon them. They can only release the unnecessary Karma for us. Unfortunately, they are not able to dissolve the Karma that we are here to work on and release as part of our spiritual growth.

Instead of having to balance 100% of the Karma we incurred, we only have to balance 51%. Forgiveness is an excellent tool to use in forgiving others for any wrongs or perceived wrongs. As we awaken to who we are and why we are here, Forgiveness becomes much easier. Again, the Lords of Karma are willing to help us release any Karma we don't need to carry.

REUNITE AS MANY SOUL FRAGMENTS AS POSSIBLE

It's difficult to reunite Soul fragments when we don't even know that parts of our Soul have left. Most people don't even think about their Soul. However, it would be a good idea to ask your Angels or Spirit Guides if any parts of your Soul exited. If so, call them back to rejoin the Soul which occupies the physical body, or ask your Angels or Spirit Guides to escort them to the parent Soul on the other side. With the mass consciousness awakening happening on Earth at this time, it is much easier to call our energy back to us or direct it to the Light. It's all about awareness. We need to know what we are expected to do. Get in the habit each day of calling back any of your own energy which may have exited throughout your day and send away, to its rightful owner, any energy you picked up that is not your own.

How to Measure Your Level of Vibration

Ascension is all about raising your energy vibration to the 5th Dimension level. This is the kindergarten level for Ascended Masters. In the next section I list numerous ways to assist in raising your vibration.

So how do we know what level of vibration we are at? When my Guides first starting giving me this information about dimensions, levels of vibration, etc., I had no idea what they were talking about. I asked them if there was a device or something on the market, like a blood pressure kit, that would measure our vibration. I thought it would be cool to bring it to my classes and let the participants measure their own levels. Unfortunately, I am not aware of any device on the market, but my Guides suggested using a twelve inch ruler (as Planet Earth consists of twelve dimensions) and a pendulum.

First, keep in mind that our spiritual vibration changes as does our blood pressure depending on what is happening in our life. Our blood pressure rises if we are exposed to trauma or stress and lowers when we are peaceful and calm. The exact opposite happens with our spiritual vibration. The more we are exposed to trauma or stress, the lower our vibration. The more peaceful and calm we are, the higher our vibration. The higher our vibration, the better life is.

Next, take a few deep breaths and let them out forcefully to calm your energy and raise your vibration.

Ask your Higher Self, Angels and/or Spirit Guides to join you and assist in measuring your vibration.

Once your spiritual assistants are with you, take the pendulum and position it at the third inch on the ruler and ask that your spiritual assistants guide and stop the pendulum at the point where your current level of vibration resides. It does not necessarily have to stop on an exact inch marker because there are many levels within each dimension.

Very slowly allow the pendulum to move upward on the ruler without forcing movement and note where it stops. It should stop at some point between inches four and seven.

If you take your blood pressure reading several times throughout the day, it is very possible you will get different readings depending on how stressed out or calm you are. The same holds true when measuring your level of vibration. Just keep in mind that the less stress, the more peaceful and calm you are, the higher your vibration will be.

For those of you who have made a connection with your spiritual guidance, all you have to do is ask them what vibration level you are at and they should be able to tell you. That is how I received my information originally. Then when I asked my guidance if there was a way we could physically measure our vibration, this is the method they suggested.

It is advisable to call in your angelic beings to assist in the measuring process, otherwise our egos could bring us up to the twelfth inch, the twelfth vibration, when that is highly unlikely.

DNA and Our Ascension

What does our DNA have to do with Ascension? EVERYTHING! When we make our Soul Plan/Contract on the other side before incarnating, we don't get a paper document to bring to Earth with us, so we have to put it somewhere. That somewhere is in our DNA. It's called a "blueprint." When we reach a certain point in life and our lessons or karmic events or the start of Ascension is scheduled to happen, triggers are activated within our DNA from our Guardians on the other side who are assigned to oversee our progress on Earth.

The Key to Ascension

Humans awakening to the fact that they are spiritual beings, Gods-in-training, is the key to Ascension. We need to awaken NOW! The Earth is on its way up and humanity needs to be ahead of Earth, as it is our vibration that is helping Earth reach Planetary Ascension. Many have incarnated, at this time, at the 5th and 6th Dimensional level of vibration for the purpose of helping the planet with its Ascension.

In other words, it is humanity that is the key to Ascension. Think of Earth as an elevator. As humans raise their vibration, the Earth ascends as well. It cannot go where it is destined to go until humans get on and push the button to the higher dimension. The elevator responds to the floors that are designated. If humanity does not get on Earth's elevator by opening their consciousness of who they are spiritually and thus raising their vibration through their thoughts, actions and deeds, the Earth's elevator was destined to stay stuck in the 3rd Dimension. Fortunately, enough humans have awakened and Earth will definitely ascend into the higher dimensions.

Earth's purpose is to serve humanity in getting to where we need to go more easily and quickly. The Earth's elevator has an automatic button that has been triggered and now it is time for it to ascend. The humans who chose not to get onto Earth's elevator to get to the next level of vibration have chosen to take the slower route – the stairway, and so they will encounter a detour in being diverted to other 3rd Dimensional planets. However, they will be able to return to Earth after they attain the 4th Dimension vibration or higher. They will be able to return to Earth to finish their Ascension Process with the rest of their Soul Group.

Chapter 16

THE ASCENSION PROCESS: SIGNS AND SETBACKS

WHILE EACH PERSON'S PROGRESS THROUGH THE Ascension Process is different, a number of signs tell us that the Ascension Process is taking place. Some of them are listed below:

✳ You become aware that you create your own reality through Free Will via your thoughts, actions and deeds.

✳ You become aware of Karma — that there are consequences for your actions. There is a misunderstanding about Karma. It is not a punishment for wrong doing. When we do our Life Review upon our return to the other side, we see and feel how we hurt others and we want to correct this, so we include the same or similar circumstances to experience in a future life in order to balance things out. We do not necessarily have to experience the circumstances with the same individuals. It is the experience and learning from it that matters. "Do unto others as you would want done unto you" is a good rule to live by to eliminate Karma in your life.

✳ You KNOW you have a purpose for being here and are anxious to do what you are supposed to be doing.

✳ The process of cleansing and purifying your physical body begins and this will be evident through the painful physical symptoms you will experience.

✳ Issues from past lifetimes and our current life surface for healing purposes. These experiences can be physically, mentally and emotionally painful as well.

✳ Relationships end or change. This is at epidemic proportion at this time. It has to do with the difference in energy vibrations. Sometimes these relationships can be reunited when the energies reach a point of greater compatibility.

✳ All of your bodies — physical, mental, emotional and spiritual — begin to align. They begin to vibrate at the same level. When the different bodies are vibrating at different levels, there is usually chaos in your life. You can assist this process by giving your intention to the Universe and asking that you want assistance in balancing all of your bodies. Bring Light from the higher dimensions (5th thru 9th) down and spin it around you like a tornado, slowing it down gradually as you repeat this statement: "As this powerful Universal energy surrounds me, I choose to release and let go of any negativity that has accumulated in any or all of my energy bodies — Physical, Mental, Emotional and Spiritual. All of my bodies are now in complete alignment. Thank You, God!"

✳   You are no longer attached to your physical and personal possessions. It's acceptable to own luxury items, but you are not emotionally attached to them. You are satisfied with what you have and trust that the Universe will provide you with whatever you NEED. "Ask and You Shall Receive!"

✳   It is no longer necessary to protect yourself from harm and or negativity, due to the Law of Attraction. Like attracts like energy. However, because of the transitional energies, it would be best to continue the practice of protecting yourself for the balance of this lifetime. This can easily be done by imagining that Light is coming from the higher dimensions in through the top of your head and filling your physical body as well as your auric field. Or you can just reach up to your spiritual guidance and ask that they protect you throughout the day.

✳   You realize that it is absolutely necessary to ground yourself as the Planet is also ascending and we need to "stick" with it. Otherwise you may feel spacey, scattered, unbalanced, dizzy, and could experience a fall. You will find a grounding exercise in Chapter

18, on page 186.

❋　You become a "lie" detector. It is so obvious when someone is lying to you. As your vibration rises, the darkness is much easier to detect. When this first started happening to me I thought, "Do they really think I am that stupid?" Now I just take the truth from conversations and leave the rest behind, rather than getting upset over the non-truths. Sometimes people get in the habit of saying what they "think" you want to hear and after a while they don't seem to realize that they are not speaking the truth.

❋　You no longer fear death. Many who have had a Near Death Experience report that they no longer fear death. As a matter of fact they look forward to it. I have not had a Near Death Experience (NDE), however, as a result of the Ascension Process, my fear of death has been dissolved.

❋　Our old beliefs and habits begin to change. Beliefs and habits which work for us at 3rd Dimension vibration are no longer appropriate when we arrive at the 4th Dimension vibration. For instance, the belief in one God is a 3rd Dimension belief. When I arrived at the 4th Dimension energy vibration, I was still not able to wrap my mind around the fact that there were many Gods. When I reached the 5th Dimension energy level, it became very clear and comfortable to understand the assumption that we are Gods-in-training. It is similar to our beliefs as children in Santa, the Easter Bunny, the Tooth Fairy, etc. These beliefs change when we get older and it's a very natural, easy transition in our beliefs.

✳   You become less judgmental of people and situations as your vibration rises. You are more in tune with the oneness theory that we are all connected through Source, yet having individual experiences. And anything each individual says, thinks or does affects all of us.

✳   You may feel and look younger than your age, or than you did before, and your friends and loved ones may mention this to you.

✳   You switch from being religious to being more spiritual.

✳   You feel less competitive and more willing to help others even if it is in the same career field. You understand that the Universe has sufficient supplies for everyone. It is no longer you against them.

✳   Your intuitive abilities are heightened automatically as a result of both your and the Earth's vibrations rising to higher levels. The veil between worlds is becoming thinner and many of us are literally living in two dimensions (4th and 5th) at the same time. It is much easier to make a connection with Spirit now than it was in the past.

✳   You experience ups and downs with your energy vibration. During the times when you are purging negative energies and emotional issues, you will feel the need to rest more often. Honor this as best you can. During the in-between times, you might experience bursts of energy where you can go night and day and not feel tired. Again, even though you may not feel tired, your body needs rest even if you are not able to fall asleep.

✳ You have an insatiable appetite for spiritual knowledge. This has happened to me. I can't seem to get enough of spiritual information. In the very beginning I asked my Spirit Guides to lead me to what I needed to know and that has worked out great for me. It's been more than twenty years, and I am more interested in learning as much as I can now than I ever was. I'm like a kid in a candy store and mommy said I can have anything I want. How exciting!

✳ We have a need and desire to connect with other like-minded individuals. Many times our family, friends, and co-workers try to dissuade us from our path if they do not understand the Ascension Process as we do. They will get there in their own time, but we need to seek out others who are having similar experiences.

✳ Being in crowds or noisy places makes us want to retreat and live in seclusion. It's the mixed and/or lower vibrating energies we are not able to tolerate. In time, as we adjust to the higher vibrating energy, this sensation will subside and we will have the desire to participate in large gatherings again.

Some Setbacks on the Path to Ascension

The Path to Ascension is not easy. We continually learn as we go through our life experiences. Many times we experience setbacks on our journey. Some of these setbacks could be:

1. Not realizing that LOVE is the most important spiritual power. Not loving yourself, God, and others (in that order).

2. Giving your personal power away by being a victim or holding power and control over others.

3. Not realizing that you CAUSE everything that is happening in your life.

4. Not eating properly or getting enough rest or exercise.

5. Not allowing joy or happiness to be a part of your life.

6. Judging others as well as yourself.

7. Being too attached to things — your possessions.

8. Giving up or giving into adversity — big trap. DON'T GIVE UP!!! Let go and let God!

9. Trying to do everything yourself and not calling upon (mentally reaching up to) God, His Angels or your Spirit Guides for help with whatever

you need.

10. Expecting God, His Angels or your Spirit Guides to do everything for you while you do nothing to help yourself.

11. Wasting too much time watching TV, violent movies, playing video games or reading "trashy" novels. While these activities may seem harmless, anything that would keep you in a negative or depressed state would not add to your spiritual growth.

Chapter 17

SYMPTOMS OF ASCENSION

DURING THE ASCENSION PROCESS, WE EXPERI-
ence physical, emotional, mental and spiritual symptoms
which are a result of the lower vibrating energies of
our carbon-based bodies transforming into the higher
vibrating energies of the crystalline Light bodies.

Please keep in mind that you will NOT experience
every one of these symptoms. Also, many symptoms
equate to commonly diagnosed medical conditions,
such as my diagnosis of Rheumatoid Arthritis. It's a
very common condition, but my guides told me the
symptoms would regress when the cells completed their
transformation process and they have.

Listed below are some of the most common Ascension symptoms:

Physical

Arms and Hands Tingling or Falling Asleep: While this is slightly uncomfortable, it doesn't last very long. It has to do with circulation.

Chronic Fatigue Syndrome and Fibromyalgia: If you are experiencing either or both of these conditions, you are definitely going through the Ascension Process. They are both relatively new diseases caused by the transformation of the cells from carbon to crystalline or Light cells.

Diarrhea: Possibly caused by the releasement of rage stored in the body. Another form of detoxification.

Digestive Disorders: Many are experiencing acid reflux, gas, bloating, etc., as a result of the quality of food they are eating — refined, processed foods are loaded with artificial ingredients and man-made chemicals and the body is not able to digest these very well. As your vibration rises, it is important to eat, healthy, raw/live, vitamin and mineral rich foods as they are higher in vibration and this is what your body needs, especially during the transformation of the cells from carbon to Light.

Dizziness: May be caused by the energy bodies spinning too fast. Grounding yourself will usually correct this condition. (See Grounding Exercise in Chapter 18, on page 186.)

Flu-like Symptoms: This is a form of detoxification

and cleansing of the body.

Gritty Eyes/Hazy Vision: Since all the physical cells are transforming, the eyes are affected as well. This is one of the symptoms I have been experiencing.

Head, Neck and Shoulder Pain: This is stored negative energy being released.

Muscle and Joint Pain: Arthritis-type symptoms usually caused by stored resistance in the body or by a "walk-in" or a rejection reaction at the cellular level. This helps in purifying and releasing blocked energy.

Night Sweats/Hot Flashes and Chills: You don't have to be pregnant, going through menopause or even female to experience these sensations. Many males have indicated that they, too, have been experiencing these symptoms. It's the transformation of the cells taking place.

Pain in the Heart Area: IMPORTANT! Whenever you experience heart pain, be sure to get immediate emergency medical attention. If the tests show that you are not experiencing a heart attack, or that you have a heart related condition, then it may be that the Heart Chakra is opening to a new level. It is a multi-dimensional gateway. Breathe Light into the heart and mentally open the Heart Chakra until the pain subsides. To open the Heart Chakra, imagine the Light energy circling very gently counter-clockwise around the Heart Chakra. You can do this procedure while waiting for medical attention.

Physical Body Vibrating: As your vibration is rising during the Ascension Process, it is natural to feel your energy vibrating. For me this felt like something was pulsating under my skin.

Nausea and Vomiting: This may be caused by fear stored in the body, which is being released.

Weight Gain and Weight Loss: The body usually gains weight before the transformation process begins, then releases weight through the "burning" process. Your weight might go up and down like a yo-yo over many years as the transformation of the cells from carbon-based to crystalline does not happen overnight.

Emotional

Anxiety/Panic Attacks: During the time when the Ego is in the process of merging with the Soul energy, the Ego does not want to let go of control so you may experience feelings of anxiety or panic.

Depression: As the dark or negative energies, which have been stored at the cellular level from this and many past lifetimes, surface you may experience feelings of depression as these energies are being purged. We cannot suppress our negative emotions indefinitely. They have to surface and be resolved or released in order to reach a higher vibration.

Disorientation: You're moving right along and all of a sudden, for a few moments, you don't know where you are. Take a few deep breaths and ground yourself. This will pass.

Emotional Ups and Downs: Crying for no apparent reason. You are just releasing negative energy. Let it out. Crying is a great cleansing process. At other times you may feel happy for no apparent reason.

Feeling Hungry/Unsatisfied: If you are eating healthy and getting proper nutrition, but still feel hungry as the food is not satisfying you, breathe in and fill your body with Light as a nutrient. Our bodies are transforming to Light Bodies so why not feed it what it needs — LIGHT!

Feeling Spacey and Out of Body: This is a very common experience and indicates that you need to ground yourself.

Fatigue and Tiredness: This is different than Chronic Fatigue Syndrome — an occasional feeling of being tired. It is important to rest whenever you can to build your energy level back up. To continue to force yourself to do what you have to do will only get you into a more chronic state of fatigue. Honor your body with "time-out," even if you think you don't have time.

Interrupted Sleep: Waking between 2:00 and 5:00 a.m. This is a great time and opportunity to connect with your Higher Self, Soul, Angels, Spirit Guides and/ or God. It may even be your Spiritual Team waking you up to communicate with you. Mentally reach up and ask if they are with you and if there is something they want to say. Then pay attention for a response. You may feel chills or goosebumps going up and down your body. They are letting you know they are with you. Take the opportunity to ask questions. Even if you don't think you are getting an answer, they will find a way of getting the message to you.

Need to Eat Often: You might experience cravings for different types of food. Many crave protein. Follow your cravings within reason.

Stress: You feel lots of pressure. It feels like the world is closing in on you. BREATHE!

Uncomfortable with the Lower Frequency Energies: You are sensitive to other people's vibration and find it very hard being in the presence of individuals who are at a lower vibration than you are. Lower vibration refers to their spiritual awareness, not that they are less than anyone else. This has caused an epidemic of relationship issues, changes and break-ups. If someone is vibrating at the 3rd dimensional vibration and they are associating with someone at the upper 4th or 5th dimensional vibration, it is very hard on both parties to remain in the relationship.

Very Vivid Dreams: You remember every detail upon waking. This is a releasement of fears and past life energies. Don't allow fear to set in as many times the dreams don't make sense. Just trust that your sub-conscious mind and Higher Self are working as you sleep to release energies that are not serving you in your growth process.

Mental

Audio Dyslexia: When someone is speaking you hear the words, but your brain can't make sense of them.

Loss of Identity: You are experiencing changes on all levels — mental, emotional, physical and spiritual and are, therefore, going through a process of creating a new identity.

Memory Loss and Trouble Accessing Words: The download of a higher vibrating energy causes this effect. It is only temporary. As your vibration raises to meet that which is being downloaded you will experience normal memory restoration.

Objects Appear to Move/Melt/Shimmer: Grounding yourself should help this condition.

Spiritual

Blowing Light Bulbs and Fuzzing Electronics: Bulbs may flicker or burn out when you are around. Your TV may appear fuzzy when you are too close to it, or your computer may malfunction. This is caused by the changes in your auric field.

Hearing Beeps/Tones/Music or Electronic "Morse Code": It may be Tinnitus or a Higher Light Vibration coming in. Just relax.

Hearing Conversations from the Other Side: The

veil between the two worlds is very thin and as your vibration rises you may be able to hear conversations at a distance. When this first started happening to me, I thought someone had left a television on in another room. Upon investigation nothing was on, and I was home alone. In my speaking with friends and clients, they have had similar experiences and thought they were going "crazy." They were happy to learn that it was part of the process of rising to higher levels.

No Desire to Eat At All: This happens when cells are burning density. Important that you eat healthy at all times, but especially during the "burning" process.

Seeing Lights: Some individuals are able to see globs of White Light as well as colored translucent lights. This is different than seeing orbs. Although orbs are very easily seen with the naked eye as well as captured by digital cameras.

Length of Symptoms

Unfortunately, there is no specific time frame for these symptoms. It is tied to our spiritual growth and raising our vibration to a higher level. Each individual is different, as we each handle our life experiences and our challenges differently. Because I resisted the process, I delayed my recovery time. The one thing that helped me through the process was to be in touch, through meditation, with my spiritual guidance who kept me informed as to what was going on and that it was not a permanent condition. Remember that if you are going through Physical Ascension, the cells are transforming by exploding and creating our Light Body. While this is a spiritual activity, we feel it physically and it can be quite painful. The Soul, the spiritual part of us, carries the pain vibration. Embrace it. Ask your guidance for whatever assistance they can provide so that you can get through it more easily. My symptoms began in January 2000 and in December 2010 I felt as though I had completed the painful part of Ascension. I was back to "normal!" While my process took 10 years, I resisted by not embracing what was happening. I only wanted it to STOP! Your process may be shorter in duration, especially if you started the process in a past life and came forward in this lifetime to complete the process.

Why Can't Our Heavenly Helpers Relieve Us of Our Pain?

Many times I have had people ask me: "If we are connected with our Spirit Guides and Angels, and they are supposed to help us, why is it necessary for us to suffer? Why can't they just take the pain away?"

There are rules associated with our pain and suffering. Since all humans agreed that we would grow spiritually through pain and suffering, our Heavenly Helpers cannot step in and take our pain away for the asking. They can, however, help relieve our pain and suffering if it is not attached to the Ascension Process, a Life Lesson or spiritual growth.

Do you know anyone who has had cancer or any life-threatening disease and they healed miraculously? While I believe in miracles, this type of situation has everything to do with the individual overcoming a challenge and the time for suffering was over. Whether we recover from an illness or we pass and return Home is all programmed in our DNA before birth.

This is an important time for growth on Planet Earth and by learning to overcome any physical, emotional, mental or spiritual challenges that are placed before us is the best "medicine" to be relieved of pain and suffering.

Chapter 18

HOW TO EASE THE PAIN & SUFFERING OF ASCENSION

THE PATH TO RAISING OUR VIBRATIONAL LEVEL and becoming an Ascended Master includes experiencing the pain and suffering of Ascension symptoms. This is part of our mission on Earth.

As mentioned in the previous chapter, many physical, mental, emotional and spiritual symptoms are caused by the Ascension Process. While these symptoms are a result of our bodies transforming from carbon to Light, there is an additional benefit to the pain and suffering that is experienced and that is to expand our abilities to love and forgive all those around us, including ourselves. This is the true path to becoming an Ascended Master.

What Can You Do to Ease the Pain and Suffering of Ascension Symptoms?

For any or all symptoms, it would be appropriate to seek traditional medical attention as many of the symptoms mimic traditional ailments. It may be necessary to take prescription drugs on a temporary basis. While I was diagnosed with Rheumatoid Arthritis, my Spirit Guides advised that I was experiencing the Ascension Process. I was not happy about taking the prescription drugs, but I have to admit they did help in relieving the pain. Many times the Ascension symptoms do not show up in the traditional testing process, such as blood tests or x-rays. In those situations, you will have to rely on your own intuition or seek alternative methods of healing.

Following are some suggestions of things you can do yourself to speed up the Ascension Process and raise the vibration of your energy. As you handle each symptom and expand your spiritual awareness to reach the level of an Ascended Master, the pain you may have been experiencing will automatically subside.

ELEMENTAL

FOOD

Alkalize the Body: Alkalizing the body is ultra important for general health reasons and also assists with the Ascension Process. To do this is just a matter of eating more of the complex carbohydrates — fresh fruits and vegetables, and less of the simple carbohydrates — sweets and processed foods. If you are not familiar with which foods are alkalizing to the body, search the Internet as there are many sites which list both the alkalizing and the acidic foods. Health food stores usually carry strips that are used to do a simple saliva test to see if your body is too acidic.

Eat Healthy Foods: It is important to eat a variety of high quality foods, especially if organic varieties are not available in your area. Processed foods will definitely lower your vibration and eventually create health issues.

You may find that you need to eat less food, and that your cravings for the "junk" food subside when you give your body what it is really craving — vitamin and mineral rich foods. Also, you may notice a craving for protein. Any source of protein you desire is acceptable. Honor what your body craves within reason.

Vitamins and Minerals

Your body needs the proper amount of vitamins and minerals through natural food sources now more than ever. If your daily diet does not allow sufficient intake of vitamins and minerals, you may want to use supplements. Be sure to purchase the highest quality supplements possible. I have found that the liquid forms are more effective than the tablet form. The healthier the cells are in your body, the easier the Ascension Process will be on you.

WATER

The body is burning the carbon-based cells and replacing them with crystalline or Light; therefore, it is important to cleanse the body of the residue by drinking lots of purified or filtered water and taking frequent baths and/or showers.

AIR

Deep Breathing: By taking in very deep breaths and letting them out forcefully you will provide oxygen to the cells. This will also assist the body in releasing tension and providing a relaxed all over feeling.

Breathing Exercise: A breathing exercise to demonstrate that deep breathing releases tension, truly relaxes you, and adds greater flexibility to your body, is as follows:

Place your feet firmly on the floor so that you have room enough to move one of your arms outward without hitting or touching anyone or anything. With feet firmly in place, take either your right or left arm and bring it up in front of you and then bring it around to the right of you if you use your right arm, or to the left if you use your left arm, all the way in back of you without putting strain on your body. Make a mental note of where your hand is pointing on the wall, doorway, window, piece of furniture, etc. Next bring your arm back and let it relax at your side. Take three very deep breaths, hold them for a count of four or five, and then let each breath out forcefully. When you finish with the third breath, open your eyes and repeat the process of bringing your arm (use the same arm you used in the beginning of this process) up in front of you and guide it around in the same direction as you did originally. Notice the distance you are able to go after deep breathing than you did when you first began the exercise. You should be able to go one to two feet further. When your body is relaxed, you have greater flexibility.

Breathing in Colors: If you are feeling fatigued, breathe in and fill your body with high vibration colors. Three high vibration colors are: red, gold, and platinum. Red has a dual purpose — high energy and passion or it can also represent anger. So if you are going to breathe in the color red, mentally put the intention out to the Universe that you are breathing it in for the purpose of higher energy within your body. Gold and platinum do not have a dual purpose. They represent positive, high energy. Again, you might want to state your intention that you are breathing these colors in and filling your body for the purpose of a higher energy level.

You can breathe in your favorite colors if you so choose, as long as you breathe them in at the highest vibration purest form possible. I sometimes use purple/violet and sometimes marble two colors together such as gold and platinum. Be guided by what feels right for you.

Earth

Stay Grounded: While the Ascension Process is causing us to rise into higher dimensions, and we feel more peaceful and calm, we are still connected to Earth. Since we are here to assist Earth in rising to a higher dimension, it is important that we stay grounded. Otherwise, we might feel spacey, experience foggy thinking and wonder if we belong here. Without grounding we might feel off-balanced and this has resulted in many individuals falling. Sometimes it is necessary to ground oneself many times throughout the day. My angels guided me to use the following simple exercise:

Grounding Exercise: Imagine that a stream of Golden/While Light is coming in through your Crown Chakra (top of the head) from the higher dimensions. Imagine that Light going through your entire body, down and out through the bottom of your feet and into the "CORE" of Mother Earth. After a few seconds bring the Light back up from the CORE of Mother Earth through the bottom of your feet, all the way up your entire body and out through the Crown Chakra and back up to the higher dimensions. This way you are connected with both Heaven and Earth at the same time. The reason it is important to go to the CORE of Mother Earth is because that is where the "mechanics" of gravity reside. With the Shift energies and the realigning of the Planet, we need to stay connected at the core or root level.

Spend Time in Nature and in the Sun: While the sun is the best source of Vitamin D with small doses of our skin being exposed directly to the sun without sun block, being in nature also has a grounding effect and helps to balance our energy and provides a peaceful atmosphere.

Personal Environment
DETOX AND CLEANSING

Detox: We need to cleanse the body, not only from the burning off of the old cells, but from the toxins we take in from food, drink, the environment, etc. We are exposed to all kinds of toxicity during our daily life, including the news, harsh music, and air pollution. Under normal conditions we can go for a long period of time before we feel the effects. However, our bodies are very vulnerable during the Ascension Process so we need to pamper ourselves and make sure we do everything possible to assist our bodies in making the transition that is necessary to ascend to higher levels.

Emotional Clearing: Many times pain and discomfort are an indication that emotional issues need to be cleared. Blocked energy can also cause pain and discomfort. The download of the higher vibrating energies is causing emotional issues to surface. You may experience this by crying for no apparent reason. However, a quick and easy way to consciously clear emotional blocks is via the Emotional Freedom Technique (EFT). This is a way of tapping on certain meridian points of the body and verbally stating the issue or situation you want to clear followed by positive affirmations to reinforce the healing process. With training you can do this yourself or go to an EFT practitioner who can help you. Emotional clearing is very important in raising your vibration.

Reduce Stress: We need to find ways to reduce the amount of stress we experience daily. As you know, stress will "zap" your energy quicker than anything. As you grow spiritually and rise to a higher vibration, you will find that the people and situations that used to cause you to lose control will not have the same effect on you anymore. You will have risen above it.

EXERCISE AND REST

Exercise: It is important that we keep our body moving. If it is too painful or you are too tired to do a regular exercise routine, just walk at whatever pace is comfortable for you. When I was bedridden and couldn't move, let alone walk, I mentally did exercises while lying in bed. I was not able to exercise at all for approximately five years and was concerned about the deterioration of my body as a result of not exercising. I couldn't even stand for more than a few minutes at a time before finding a place to sit down. Remembering that our thoughts create our reality, I practiced self-hypnosis and exercised my body mentally while lying in bed. I believed that this would help me, and I guess it did as my muscles did not turn to mush. So whatever you need to do to get your body moving — do it!

Proper Amount of Sleep: This is actual sleep time. Seven to eight hours is appropriate even if it is interrupted sleep. This is different from rest or the little "naps" we may take during the day. Again, the body regenerates and heals during sleep time.

Rest: The body is going through a major transformation and it needs a lot of rest to recuperate. The body was designed with a built-in self-healing mechanism, but we have to do our part in assisting it to heal itself and rest is extremely important. Many individuals, including myself, have had to take "naps" during the day when we never had to do this before. This is fine. It does not mean that you are lazy or ill; it is as simple as the body needs time to restore itself. Sometimes ten to twenty minutes will be sufficient and sometimes you need to rest for a few days or more. The human way is that we have to be busy every waking moment, and this is not appropriate during the Ascension Process.

Resistance Causes Pain

Do Not Resist the Process: Fear and resistance only create unpleasant experiences resulting in more discomfort. When I was in so much pain I didn't know what to do, my Guides and Angels kept telling me not to resist. I had no idea what they were talking about as I was lying in bed unable to move. How could I be resisting?

I was in the "victim" mode of poor me. Why do I have to go through this pain and suffering? I'm a good person. I help other people. I'm doing God's work. Why me! That was the resistance! I was keeping myself stuck with that type of thinking. Once I got out of that mode and followed the spiritual advice of wrapping the areas of my body that were throbbing with pain with the LOVE vibration, things got much better. Using the Love Vibration as a healing tool is very similar to using the Light, the Universal or God's energy vibration. My Angels suggested I use God's LOVE vibration, and I received almost instant gratification. It is your intention and belief that surrounding yourself with God's Love energy will bring healing that is the "magic." If you perform this intentional visualization and think that "It won't work," then it won't work for you. Let go and allow your Spiritual Team to do as you ask.

I had good days and bad days. One day I had a party to go to for the Christmas holiday. I prayed and asked that I have a good day on the day of the party so I could enjoy myself. I woke up with a migraine-type headache. I had never had a migraine before and very seldom ever got a headache. My first reaction was anger. I had asked to be pain-free. What happened to "Ask and You Shall Receive?" After deciding that there was no way I could go to the party, I laid my head back on the pillow and the reminder thought came to me about wrapping the painful area with the LOVE vibration. I had nothing to lose so I tried it. Within five minutes the headache was gone completely, and I was up and getting dressed to go to the party.

I struggled so much with resistance for many years. It was my own fault as I did not listen — I resisted. Once I got out of the victim mode and decided to do what I could to help myself in any way that I could, the resistance stopped. I thank my Guides and Angels for helping me to realize that LOVE is the answer to all of our prayers. This was a hard lesson for me because when you are in so much pain it is hard to think in terms of the LOVE vibration. But it does work. Even though we all have a tremendous amount of spiritual guidance available to us in the Spirit World, our helpers cannot learn our lessons for us and they cannot do anything to interfere with our growth. They can guide and advise us, but our Free Will decisions override any guidance they may provide, as it is our experience, not theirs. They have to step back and let us do what we want to do.

Spiritual Practices

Trust: Know that you have a spiritual team on the other side overseeing the Ascension Process. After you have called them in and asked for their assistance, let go and allow them to do their work. As stated in the above example, do not RESIST their help. They will do anything within their power to help us as long as it is spiritually legal. We need to ask and then allow them to do what they can on our behalf.

All Forms of Energy Healing: Any form of energy or hands-on healing where the practitioner is using Universal Energy as the healing force. When I was not able to get out of bed, my Angels and Guides suggested that I bring God's Love and Light vibration down from the higher dimensions and mentally massage it into the areas where I was experiencing pain. I just wanted them to take the pain away. I had suffered long enough. However, when I tried their suggestion, the pain subsided in a matter of minutes. If visualizing the massaging process does not work for you, then go ahead and do a hands-on massage if that works better. How long you do this process is up to you. You will automatically know when to stop if you connect with your spiritual guidance as they will direct you.

Communicate with Your Soul: We tend to want to be in control and end up getting in our own way. Step aside and let your Soul guide you to a smoother and easier transition. Remember, part of the Ascension Process is to integrate the personality/ego part of ourselves with the Soul and allow the Soul to guide us along our journey here on Earth. The ego does not know the way to enlightenment. The Soul has the blueprint, and can guide us to where we need to be much quicker and easier.

Connect With Your Angels and Spirit Guides: Again Angels and Spirit Guides are assigned to us before birth for the purpose of helping us achieve our goals. By connecting with them and allowing them to provide guidance, it makes the process much easier. Meditation is a valuable tool in connecting with all of your spiritual team.

Connect With Your Higher Self: After you have integrated the personality/ego part of you with your Soul, it is time to reach up to your Higher Self for guidance. The Higher Self is the Spirit part of us — the Oversoul. Through meditation you will be able to receive information to help guide you along your path and to know where you are on the path of Ascension. You are at the 5th dimensional level of vibration when you are able to connect with your Higher Self.

Positive Thinking: Our thoughts create our reality. So if we dwell on the pain and discomfort we are experiencing, we will stay stuck in that reality. If we concentrate on being free of pain, then we will create a new reality. Negative thinking was a habit for me. It took many years for me to get in the habit of switching negative thoughts to positive thoughts. Negative thinking is a habit, and it can be broken like any other habit, but it takes effort. As an exercise for one day, consciously practice overriding your negative thoughts with positive thoughts. You will be amazed at how the mind loves negativity. I still have moments where I find myself in the negative mode, but it is quicker and easier to correct now.

Listen to Classical and Other High Frequency Music: This will relax your body and mind and soothe your Soul. It also attracts your Angels and Spirit Guides.

Prayer and Meditation: During quiet or rest time, make a habit of praying and meditating. A segment of Ascension is to connect with our Spiritual Team on the other side, and it will give those who feel they "have" to be doing something, something to do that will benefit and assist them with spiritual growth.

Visualization: During meditation, visualize yourself getting into an elevator and going to the 5th Dimension or higher. Call your Higher Self, Angels or Spirit Guides to join you at whatever Dimension they feel is appropriate for you. The elevator will stop at the appropriate dimension; the doors will open and your Guides will be there to greet you. Then spend some time in the vibration of that dimension — soak it up like a sponge and bring it back to Earth with you. When this is done on a regular daily basis, you will not only assist in your own healing process, but you will also raise your level of vibration.

Bring Joy into Your Life: Very important! Do something fun! Treat yourself to something special! Enjoy yourself! Be kind to yourself! If you can do for others, you can do for yourself. No room for guilt. You should treat yourself on a regular basis because you deserve it, and it will make you feel GOOD!

Secrets of the Fifth Dimension

One of the reasons why the above suggestions will ease the pain and suffering of the Ascension Process is that they will raise our level of vibration. A "SECRET" that many people do not know is that when we reach the 5th dimensional level of vibration on a 24/7 basis, we will be free of the pain and suffering from the Ascension Process. We will have risen above it by entering the vibration of the Ascended Masters.

Chapter 19

MEDITATION

WHILE I BRIEFLY MENTIONED MEDITATION IN the previous chapter to assist with relieving pain and suffering from the Ascension symptoms, I want to further expand on the overall benefits of meditation that have helped me raise my vibration, connect to my spiritual helpers, and receive answers to my personal questions.

Many believe that meditation is a spiritual practice. I admit the reason I got involved with meditation many years ago was to help me connect with my spiritual guidance. It is one of the best practices I engage in to help know if I am following my path. While meditation may not be for everyone, there are many individuals receiving guidance from above without the process of meditation or even knowing where the information is coming from.

In addition to the spiritual benefits, meditation

offers many additional benefits for the mind and body. Some of these are:

* Lowers Stress
* Decreases Blood Pressure
* Relieves Pain
* Boosts the Immune System
* Reduces Fear, Anxiety, Anger, Depression
* Creates Balance between the Left and Right Brain
* Increases Mental Clarity/Memory and Concentration/Focus
* Improves Learning Abilities
* Increases Intuitive Abilities and Creativity
* Activates the Self-Healing Mechanism in the Body
* Alleviates Insomnia
* Lowers Oxygen Use
* Creates a Peaceful/Calm Inner Sense of Well-Being
* Resolves Inner Conflict

Meditation and Heavenly Helpers

Meditation is the key to connecting with the inner self and heavenly helpers — Soul, Higher Self, Spirit Guides and Angels. A daily practice of meditation, even for a few minutes, can bring peace and happiness and add to the quality of life. When working in the corporate world, stress was part of the daily routine. Engaging in the practice of meditation caused my stress levels to decrease dramatically.

An extra bonus for me was that meditation helped me through menopause with the greatest amount of ease. I only experienced occasional irritability and two or three hot flashes. For me it was unexpected and unbelievable. I remember my mother suffering terribly with the symptoms of menopause. The only thing I did differently was meditation.

Time to Meditate

It is important to establish a daily ritual of meditation even if you can only devote five to ten minutes. Eventually it will expand into fifteen or thirty minutes and then into an hour. The deeper the state of altered consciousness you are able to achieve, the longer your meditation will be. It will allow you to have a better control of your life and to direct your actions in a more positive manner rather than reacting negatively to stressful situations.

Different Types

There are many different types of meditation. No one method is better than another. Be guided to what feels right for you. In the beginning, I was not able to settle down and relax, so I listened to some guided relaxation audio tapes and CDs. Now I just close my eyes, surround myself with Golden White Light for protection, take some deep breaths, hold to the count of four, and then let them out forcefully. When I feel relaxed, I imagine that I am at the ocean on a beautiful sunny day, with white puffy clouds sprinkled throughout the deep blue sky and a gentle breeze. You can imagine any setting that is comfortable for you — in a meadow of flowers and green grass, by a brook, stream or lake, in the forest or even in the desert.

There are four levels of the mind:

Beta: Conscious "thinking" alert state. We go throughout our work day at this level. While not the best state for meditation for the beginner, I have been able to receive some really good information during my daily activities.

Alpha: Relaxed, semi-conscious state. This is good for meditation, especially for beginners.

Theta: Very relaxed deep trance state. This level is a more advanced state for meditation. We are able to reach higher dimensions in the Spirit World and receive more detailed information.

Delta: Unconscious, sleep state.

Toss Out Personal Questions

Create your own peaceful and sacred space in your mind and include anything to make it comfortable for you. Then mentally toss out questions you want answers to. If you have not connected with your spiritual partners and have no desire to do so, this is fine. Just toss the questions out and allow the responses to come in a way that is appropriate for you. Sometimes they come through other people, or in a flash of insight. It does not matter. Just relax, allow and be comfortable with asking. I guarantee your life will get better as you allow the inner self (Soul) to connect with the outer self (Higher Self) in guiding you in the direction you need to go. Some of the most successful people in the world do not necessarily engage in a formal meditation practice, but they do listen to that inner voice.

I find the best time for me to receive answers to my own personal questions is just before falling asleep at night. Many times I do go into the Delta state before receiving my answers, but they are delivered to me the next day in some form, either through another person, listening to the radio or television, or seeing an ad in a magazine. There is an endless list of ways our spiritual guidance can get messages to us, but we have to pay attention and be ready to recognize the answers no matter in what form they arrive.

Chapter 20

MESSAGES FROM THE ASCENDED MASTERS

BECOMING AN ASCENDED MASTER IS PART of the evolutionary process. We are classified as an Ascended Master when our vibration reaches the beginning level of the 5th Dimension. Each lifetime, as we learn the lessons we put into our Life Plan, we grow to higher spiritual levels. The growth results from overcoming the challenges that are placed before us, by our turning negative situations into positive outcomes.

Few before us have reached this level on an individual basis. Now that we are able to achieve Ascended Master status in group or mass form, many have chosen this lifetime to ascend. If it is programmed in our DNA to become an Ascended Master in this lifetime, circumstances are set up with the assistance of our Heavenly

Helpers for us to accomplish this mission.

Forgiveness of self and others, compassion for all, as well as raising our capacity to love self and others as God loves all of us, no matter what is going on and no matter how much someone may have hurt us, will release any emotional baggage we may be carrying from this lifetime and past lifetimes. This will lead us to the path to Ascension.

Some of the Ascended Masters that I work with have agreed to come forward and provide comments regarding their Ascension. Following are messages from my Master Guide Jonathan, St. Germain, Sananda and Lord and Lady Arcturus.

Message from Jonathan

Many of the lifetimes I had on Earth were filled with struggle and much negativity, so I took the easy way out. I decided to earn my "wings" on this side, in the Spirit World, by helping others. It is the mission of acting as a Master Guide to this beautiful Soul called Barbara that I attained Ascended Master status. I was very close to this vibration when I returned from Earth on my last journey. However, I did not quite make it to the 5th Dimension vibration.

My message to anyone who does not make the Ascended Master level in this lifetime is that you have two choices: Incarnate once again and make another attempt, which will be successful, or stay on this side and assist another human to achieve Ascended Master status on Earth.

~ Jonathan

Message from St. Germain

Becoming an Ascended Master was not an effort I made consciously. My growth brought me to a level of vibration where I felt very powerful, not the ego-type powerful, but the God-type sense of power. I often imagined what it would be like to be God. It seemed impossible to ever know. But on this particular day, while still on Earth, a wonderful, loving, happy feeling came over me and I knew, I knew for sure, that this was the way that God feels all the time. God did not have bad days or bad moods. He only has good, happy days. That is the way I wanted to feel all the time. It was at that moment that my spiritual guides told me that I was at the Ascended Master vibration and that is why I was feeling so good. During the balance of my days on Earth, I felt that same wonderful feeling about seventy-five percent of the time. During the balance of time, I was a victim of the negativity that was all around me. It is worth the effort to keep bringing yourself back into a positive mindset, whenever you feel negativity creeping in, no matter what the cause. God bless you all!

~St. Germain

Message from Sananda

Please know that it is possible for me to watch over all of you. I am with you even if you don't believe in me. I am one with you and one of you. We are the same. Your belief in me is not mandatory as when you return Home to this side, you will realize that we are friends. As this messenger (Barbara) told you of her experience in asking for help and told you that you, too, have the same right and power to do the same. She is correct. However, do not ask until you truly want help. We can see; we know the truth of really wanting help and only asking because you feel that someone else can fix your problems. No one but you can fix your Soul. You are in charge of nurturing your Soul and you can do this through your Free Will decisions in life.

I became an Ascended Master during my lifetime as the entity you all know as Jesus. When I entered life on Earth at that time, I entered as a world leader and teacher, and through my thoughts, actions and deeds I rose to the Ascended Master level. God has revised the requirements so that all of humanity will be able to reach the Ascended Master status much more easily now.

God's plan is for all of humanity to reach the Ascended Master vibration and beyond through the evolutionary process. You have many Souls cheering for you than you can imagine. On Earth, when many hundreds or thousands of individuals attend a concert or a sports event and they are happy with the performance, they stand up and applaud. Well, you all have a cheering section here in the Spirit World that you cannot see or hear, but they are there cheering you on with your progress.

Know that you are never alone no matter how difficult life circumstances seem to be. If you are calling out to us in time of need and you think we do not hear, know that we are aware of your needs, but according to the terms of your contract there is something you need to learn and we cannot step in and make things right. We can only assist you when you are ready to move forward. We are with you all the time so we ask that you acknowledge our efforts by doing the very best you can to reach the highest spiritual level possible.

Be at peace and KNOW that you are loved!
~Sananda

Message from the Arcturians

The type of bliss, freedom, and all-knowing that humans can evolve to as a result of these energy shifts is beyond comprehension. We are operating from Star energy and are very grateful to be assisting humanity at this special time in Earth's history.

We were human beings during the early days of Earth and have evolved to this level. Our message to humanity is to stay true to oneself. Stay true to your beliefs. If those beliefs change in time, know that is part of the evolutionary process. We are speaking from experience. We remember that life on Earth was not easy, but we also know that the benefits of evolution are worth every second of suffering that is endured. Keep in mind, the degree or level of suffering by humanity is a personal choice and the choice is through your Free Will. At this point, the Free Will should have had enough of suffering and, therefore, Ascension is the next phase. We are with you on your Path to Ascension. Feel free to reach up and ask for our assistance should you feel the necessity. We are commissioned by the God of your planet to assist humanity, and it is our honor and pleasure to do so.

Ascension blessings to you all.
    ~Lord and Lady Arcturus

The Key to Future Lifetimes

Remember that this lifetime is the key to future lifetimes. If you achieve the 4th Dimension vibration, you will be able to reincarnate on planet Earth in the future to achieve Ascended Master status. If you remain at the 3rd Dimension vibration, you will have to incarnate on other 3rd Dimensional planets until such time as you reach the 4th Dimension vibration. Then you will be able to return to Earth. I honestly don't believe anyone interested in reading this book is at the 3rd Dimension vibration.

Even though I have reached the Ascended Master status, I am told by my Guides that I have programmed one more lifetime in physical form to help other Souls in my group reach the Ascended Master vibration. There are many here on Earth now who have reached the Ascended Master status, but have chosen not to return again. There are also many who came into physical form this lifetime at the Ascended Master vibration for the sole purpose of assisting humanity and Planet Earth on our journey to a higher dimension. I say: "Thank You" to all of you.

PART IV

CREATING HEAVEN ON EARTH

Chapter 21

INTERPRETATION OF THE LORD'S PRAYER

JESUS GAVE US THIS PRAYER AS PART OF HIS Sermon on the Mount. We have recited this prayer many times like a mantra, but how many of us have taken the time to analyze what it really says? Below is a very simple interpretation given to me by Jesus/Sananda, where he is affirming to God our mission of Creating Heaven on Earth:

Our Father who art in Heaven — Jesus is addressing God from Earth in an informal manner as a parental figure, on behalf of all of humanity through the use of the word "Our."

Hallowed be thy name — Even though Jesus addressed God informally, He is expressing respect and reverence through the use of the word "hallowed."

Thy Kingdom come — God's Kingdom has been brought to Earth through the spark of Divine Light within each of us.

Thy Will be done — God's Will/Plan will be carried out through humanity.

On Earth as it is in Heaven — Jesus is affirming to God humanity's mission for being on Earth — to create Heaven on Earth.

Give us this day our daily bread — Jesus is asking that God provide us with the basic human needs. Once we reach the Ascended Master vibration, manifesting our heart's desires will be very easy. No matter what our circumstances, if we remember to reach up and ask God for what we need, it will be provided to us. Remember that God works through his Earth Angels (other humans) in providing our needs. The reason we have to ask is because of the gift of Free Will. "Ask and you shall receive." I have found this to be so true after struggling for years to make things happen through my own efforts. It's much easier to ASK! The higher your vibration, the quicker you will reap the benefits.

And forgive us our trespasses, as we forgive those who trespass against us — Forgiveness is one of the "survival" tools God has given humanity, and Jesus is asking God to forgive us and we, in turn, will forgive those who have hurt us.

And lead us not into temptation — Because we got

caught up/stuck in our humanness, Jesus is asking God to lead us away from this path.

But deliver us from evil — He is asking God to set humanity free, to liberate us from the path of darkness we were following at that time.

For thine is the Kingdom, and the Power, and the Glory forever — This statement is affirming that God's Kingdom and all His Power and His Glory will last forever. This line was not spoken by Jesus in the original Lord's Prayer. It was added later, and is simply giving praise to God before the ending of the prayer.

Amen — Usually means the ending of the prayer, but could also mean "So Be It!"

Teacher and Ascended Master

Jesus came to Earth over 2,000 years ago at the Teacher vibration. He exited that lifetime as an Ascended Master. He came to show all of humanity the way back Home to God, Our Father. He was somewhat ahead of His time as most of humanity was not ready to accept his teachings.

Many of us have been awakening slowly at first, but now with the energy shifts things have accelerated and we are more than ready to do as Jesus and other Christed entities have done to reach the higher spiritual vibrations. There is such a difference in how you feel, act and think when you release the negativity which has accumulated at the Soul level during so many lifetimes.

The Second Coming of Christ

The Second Coming of Christ refers to the awakening of the Christ Consciousness on Earth. It does not mean that Jesus plans to reincarnate in physical form and return to Earth. Those who have achieved the Christ Consciousness level are working with us from the other side to help us reach the higher vibration of an Ascended Master. As I've said before, even though it may not "appear" so, this is a wonderful time to be on Earth. We are making history.

The time is NOW for humanity to bring Heaven to Earth through that spark of Divine Light we carry within. When you have occasion to recite the Lord's Prayer, you may want to add your own personal message to God, Our Father, before you say "Amen," such as "Dear God, I AM willing to do my part in bringing Heaven to Earth. PLEASE HELP ME!"

Chapter 22

A PEEK AT LIFE ON EARTH IN THE FUTURE

WHAT I HAVE BEEN TOLD BY MY SPIRITUAL guidance is that life in our distant future will be similar to what we now consider science fiction. It has already been happening on a very small scale, but will become the norm eventually.

Major Areas Where Change Is Needed

My guidance tells me that reform needs to take place in five major areas: Government, Financial, Medical, Education and Religion. What else is left? This is not just within the United States, but worldwide. Eventually there will be one World Government and one World Religion. What form of government or what religion, or how long this will take, I do not know. It seems impossible at this time, but I have faith that God's plan will somehow come into being when the time is Divinely right with our help, of course. Again, because the majority of people on Earth will be vibrating at a much higher level, we won't have to worry about corruption as it exists in today's world.

THE HIGHER OUR VIBRATION, THE BETTER OUR LIFE

The higher our vibration rises, the easier and more peaceful life will be. Our connection with God and the Universe will be much stronger than it is now. We will have the ability to heal ourselves and manifest whatever we want and need instantaneously. If you desire luxury items, and they will make you happy, there is no harm in having them. It is not wrong to want to pamper yourself or to want to surround yourself with things that bring joy into your life. As long as you do not obtain them through illegal means and do not become attached or possessive of them, then go ahead and enjoy.

BY-PASSING THE BIRTHING PROCESS

In the future, the more highly advanced Souls who choose to spend time on Earth will be spared having to go through the birthing process, going to school to be educated, and getting a job to be able to fulfill their mission in life. They will be able to manifest a physical body and whatever else they need for the time they will be on Earth. Their purpose for coming into physical form will be to help other humans accelerate their growth to be able to evolve into the higher Dimensions. They will be able to do what they came here to do with complete awareness of what that is and then return to the other side when they are done serving humanity. No "death," no funeral — just good-bye!

As a first step on this path, Walk-Ins are by-passing the birthing process in order to fulfill their mission in an already existing human body. This is being done by contract only, so don't worry about your body being taken over by a Walk-In. That will not happen.

Those who will have the ability to manifest a physical body without going through the birthing process will have the advantage of living life multi-dimensionally. If they choose to vacation on another planet or galaxy or universe, they will be able to do so. It will be a gift for them as a result of having achieved a higher vibration and serving Earth in physical form.

Our Mission to Humanity

During the time when the spiritual part of us is at a high vibration, and we are able to journey to Earth in our spiritual body, create an appropriate physical body and do whatever we need to do, we will only have the highest best interest in mind for our fellow soul humans. ***Our mission will be only to help and not hurt humanity.***

GOVERNMENT

Once we are able to appear and disappear at will, won't the governments of the world have fun trying to keep track of the "illegal aliens" for tax and census purposes? Our angels see the humor in this situation, as control is something that has gotten out of hand with many governments on Earth at this time. Control is fine when the intent is to help fellow humans or to organize large groups of individuals. However, control, when it is taken away from the many and given to a few power-hungry individuals who thrive by intimidating and making others feel inferior is not in the highest best interest of all. We will see a major change in most governments on Earth by the year 2040. It will be necessary for those in power to reach up to the higher realms for assistance and, when that happens, life on Earth will be much better and easier for all. And, more importantly, it will be a fair system where all will be treated equally.

COMPUTER CHIP IMPLANT:
AN URGENT WORD OF CAUTION FROM SANANDA

After the September 11, 2001 attacks in New York City and Washington, DC, in the United States there was speculation that it might be necessary to have a computer chip type device implanted, possibly in our wrist area, for identification purposes. This was supposed to protect us from future terrorist attacks. The spiritual beings on the other side see things differently than what was presented to us. They warn that if we agree to this identification implant we have kissed our freedom and our rights good-bye. Sananda has indicated on several occasions that we need to speak up if we do not like what our elected officials are contemplating. So if we are given a vote on the identification implant, follow the advice of your Heart, Soul and spiritual guidance before making your decision.

EDUCATION

Regarding education, the big change here will be that children will be placed in classes according to their abilities and not by their ages as is done now. There will be a special testing system and depending on the test results, a six year-old could be placed in the sixth grade or higher. The Earth is receiving many advanced Souls and they are bored in school under the current system. The Indigo Children (highly advanced/vibrating Souls) are here to change the education system, whether they know it or not, among other things. Albert Einstein was one of the first Indigo Children to come to Earth. He was classified as an "idiot" incapable of learning. I guess he showed the "experts." He was a highly advanced Soul, here for a purpose and was bored in the classroom so he spent his time gazing out the window up to the heavens. When it was time for him to serve humanity, he did what he was here to do. This is an example of why we shouldn't judge others. We don't know what their purpose is, and things aren't always as they appear.

HEALTH ISSUES

In the immediate future, there will be a necessity for traditional medical doctors to consider adding the following to their patient care services:

* Natural and Alternative Healing combined with traditional medicine.
* Nutritional Counseling.
* Medical Intuitive to assist with and/or confirm diagnosis and treatment.

This is already being done to some extent because of the demand for natural, healthy healing methods, but eventually the prescription pads will have to go. No longer are the medical researchers looking for ways to "cure" illnesses. They are more interested in covering them up with drugs that cause other problems, which often need another prescription.

As the majority of humans reach higher and higher vibrational levels, there will be less and less need for traditional medical treatments. The body was designed to be a self-healing mechanism, and we will return to the original healing blueprint of depending upon the natural and so-called alternative healing methods for most common ailments.

FUTURE OF RETIREMENT

There has been talk for several years about the Social Security system in the U.S. going bankrupt. Whether there is truth to this or not, I don't know. However, the plan for our future (worldwide) is to live in communities and the community leaders would be responsible for taking care of and looking after the needs of those in their community. It seems that our ancestors followed this plan before Social Security came into existence. Sananda has indicated on several occasions that we, the people, need to stand up to our elected officials and voice our opinion as to how they are governing us and not just accept whatever happens with an "oh well" attitude. This holds true in individual situations as well. If someone is manipulating or "bullying" us, we need to stand up for ourselves.

BEYOND FOOD

As more and more humans raise their level of vibration, they will have the option of eating food or not. There are some 100,000+ individuals on the planet at this time who have already achieved this level. When my Spirit Guides directed me to information on Breatharians, they strongly indicated that this was for information purposes only. I was NOT ready and should not attempt to become one. Breatharians survive on getting what their body needs from the Universe through the breath. An individual could definitely die since their organs would shut down from going without food and water if they were not spiritually ready. I love food and eating too much to give it up. However, as humanity evolves spiritually, this will become a more common practice. The only Breatharian I personally knew was Dr. Joshua David Stone. He said that most societies and cultures in the world revolve around socializing with food and drink and that it was awkward to not indulge.

God's Plan for Cleaning Up the Planet

When this lifetime is over, Souls that have not reached the 4th Dimension level of vibration will not be able to reincarnate on planet Earth. They will be assigned to other planets which are still at the 3rd Dimension level of vibration. Humans will not find it very comfortable on these other 3rd Dimension planets. It is my understanding that they will not have Free Will at these other locations and that Earth is "the cream of the crop" planet because of its mission to bring Heaven to the physical world, and we are in the process of creating that now.

Once a Soul who has been assigned to another 3rd Dimension planet reaches the 4th Dimension level of vibration, it will be able to return to Earth to continue its growth with the rest of their Soul Group.

There is still time. I have outlined many things that can be done to raise your vibration, such as switching negative thoughts to positive thoughts, being willing to forgive others and yourself, showing compassion for all of God's creations, and expanding your capacity to love unconditionally no matter how things appear to be. So it is up to you. The effort is truly worth it and you will reap the rewards, not only here on Earth, but in the higher dimensions when you return after physical death.

As a result of lower vibrating Souls not being allowed to incarnate on Earth, terrorism and corruption will diminish significantly. This will not happen immediately, but gradually over the next hundred years. Be patient. It will all unfold in Divine Time. Once our Souls reach the 5th, 6th and 7th levels of vibration, we will begin to experience Heaven on Earth. Each individual will have this experience in their own time. They could go to bed one night and wake up the next morning and realize that they are experiencing Heaven on Earth. Some have already experienced this feeling.

AFTER THE 2012 ENERGY SHIFTS

After the 2012 energy shifts, the planet will have much to be thankful for. All the prayers that humans are saying in order to save the planet will have a profound effect, not only on the future of our planet but also on the evolution of humanity.

Many, many hundreds of thousands of individuals are reaching the point of awakening. They are curious as to whether there is more to life than life itself. Is there truly an afterlife? And if so, what is this afterlife like? The answers to all the questions these individuals have will be available through the forerunners on the Path to Ascension. The answers are within each and every human, but the curious ones will not be sure that they have the "right" answers so they will be looking to the more spiritually advanced Souls on Earth for direction. These advanced Souls were the pioneers along this Path to Ascension and have come to Earth at this particular time in history to assist those who are now "waking" up. The effect of helping those who awaken later will snowball throughout every lifetime until each and every human has reached the beginning level of Ascension — 5th Dimension level of vibration which is the kindergarten level for Ascended Masters.

Once a planet shifts to a higher dimension, the occupants living there, whether they are occupying the human, animal, plant or mineral kingdoms will have to leave if they have not reached the 4th Dimension level of vibration. While my spiritual guidance has not provided me with information regarding the mineral, plant and animal kingdoms on Earth, I understand that some species will be exiting and other higher vibrating species will enter. This is part of the evolutionary process. The higher the vibration of the planet and all of its occupants, the more peaceful it will become. This is God's Plan for bringing Peace on Earth and bringing Heaven and Earth together as one vibration. This was the original plan and it still remains in effect and will until this mission is accomplished. Can God do it all by Himself? Absolutely! However, the plan is for humans to do this as Gods-in-training. Once each Soul extension rises in vibration and connects with its Oversoul, and all the Oversouls blend together and return to the Monad, then we will be done with our co-creating training. At that point we will be able to create our own Universe with as many planets as we feel our Universe will need. Each will have a diversity that you can't even imagine at this time.

EXTREME FUTURE

Regarding the extreme future for planet Earth, once all Souls have completed their mission and there is no longer a need for Soul growth, it will not be necessary for Earth to exist as a physical planet any longer. At that time, it will self-destruct (explode) and become a Star. Do not be upset over this as it is the natural evolution of each planet and has been going on for multi-millions of years. This is not scheduled to happen for eons of time, and most likely the planet will be void of physical life.

Life in non-physical form exists on certain stars, although not on all stars. Some stars have been created for the purpose of adding Light and beauty to the galaxy which is a more important purpose than you can imagine. A star serves the entire galaxy of the Universe it belongs to, not just one specific planet. So stars have a very important role within the composition of the Universe. When Earth becomes a star, all the negativity will have transformed into Light energy for the good of all. Earth will be a star which maintains non-physical spiritual life.

Star Energy

Star energy is much greater, more powerful than the energy generated by a planet. Also, life in non-physical form is not only possible, but does exist on many of the stars we view in the nighttime sky from planet Earth. Arcturus is only one example. Life which exists within the star energy is governed by two individuals who consist of a male and female energy for balance. The Souls who choose to follow the leadership of an individual star act as group energy, while maintaining their individual identities. Whatever identity they have experienced in the past from physical lifetimes can be brought forward to the star existence. So we will have the best of both worlds — our own individual identity, as well as operating from the powerful group energy.

The End of Old Ways and Habits

Many fear that the world might come to an end during the 2012 energy shifts. I do not share this fear as I believe it is only the end of humanity's old ways and habits that are ego and fear-based.

Even though it may "appear" that the world is coming to an end, it truly is just the beginning of a new way of life — the type of life that we all dream about having "someday." That "someday" is just about here and it will take the collective effort of multi-millions of humans to bring it about for the masses. December 21, 2012 will be just another day as the energies have been being downloaded for many years now, since 1950, very gradually at first and now they are accelerated into high speed. So we can either "get on Earth's elevator" with the majority of our fellow human beings or we can take the alternate route and stay at a lower vibration and after this lifetime find ourselves on another planet to continue our growth before being able to return to Earth. Wouldn't it be better to be one of the ones creating Heaven on Earth instead of returning after it has already manifested without your help?

I encourage all of you to recognize the special God being that you are. Not one of us is more special than another. We are just playing different roles. It's time to let your Light shine and to become the Ascended Master that you are destined to be. This is your destiny; if not during this lifetime, it will happen in a future lifetime — guaranteed! The times of pain, suffering and struggle will end, but only with your conscious efforts through your thoughts, actions and deeds. Keep them positive no matter what is happening around you, and you will witness miracles taking place in your life.

AFTERWORD

As I review my spiritual journey, the processes of Awakening and Ascension were not easy for me as I had to deal with a lot of negativity. Self-imposed negativity, as I was looking at life from the wrong perspective. The glass was always half empty instead of being half full. So it took me a little longer than my Life Plan called for as a result of my getting in my own way. It doesn't have to be that hard for those who are in the process of opening up at this time. The energy being downloaded to Earth is at a higher vibration, more powerful than before, to assist humanity and Earth with the Ascension process.

To reiterate, humanity's ultimate purpose is to create Heaven on Earth. We are doing this through our spiritual growth. Our spiritual growth results in our achieving a higher vibration through our thoughts, actions, and deeds.

The Awakening Process begins with our search for TRUTH — a search for God. When life is super good in every area but we are still not happy, this is a sign that the Soul is anxious to get on its path and to do what it is destined to do while here. We realize that we are not just human beings; more importantly, we are spiritual beings. With the Awakening Process our vibration increases. This is spiritual growth.

After the Awakening Process, then the Ascension Process begins. The cells in the physical body go through a spiritual transformation from carbon-based to crystalline, creating a Light body. As the density of the carbon-based cells is released, more Light energy is able to occupy the cells; this, too, will increase our vibration. When our spiritual body is vibrating at the low end of the 5th Dimension, we are classified as Ascended Masters at the Kindergarten level. Life gets much easier and proceeds much quicker when we reach this level.

In this book, I have not included information regarding "Earth Changes" as a result of the Energy Shifts of 2012. All you have to do is watch and listen to the news to know that there are earth changes going on all over the world. Others have made predictions on this subject. However, since my guidance had not provided me with any information, I asked if they had anything they wanted to say on that subject. Their response was:

"Earth changes, to some degree, have always taken place on Earth. However, because of the shift of the planet into a higher dimension, these changes will take place more frequently."

I am not aware of which areas are scheduled for natural disasters. I only know what Spirit has shared with me; and that is, when the human body takes in something that is hard or impossible to digest, it has to get rid of it in some manner, such as vomiting or diarrhea, in order for the body to right itself and balance the digestive process. It has to eliminate that which is causing the problem. Earth is a God-created living entity and, therefore, needs to vomit/purge through natural disasters in order to move forward and upward to the higher dimension. We can assist ourselves as well as Mother Earth by releasing and letting go of the negativity we have accumulated, not only during this lifetime, but also from many past lives in order for our Ascension to take place.

My angelic friends have said that it is not necessary to worry or look for a "safe" place to live during these turbulent times, as the safety net resides in our DNA. If an individual is programmed to leave this planet at a particular time, it does not matter where they are located. There is no safe place. Those who are to survive will be safe no matter where they live. This is not doom and gloom. It is a decision that was made by each Soul before coming into physical form.

Part of the survival process is human helping human during these turbulent times. There is massive spiritual growth connected with individuals stepping up to help during any type of emergency situation. Do what you can do, whether it is helping through physical labor, financially through donations, or spiritually through prayers for all those affected by the disasters.

Even though we appear to be separate, we are all part of the ONE Source energy. And we ultimately all have the same purpose — to create Heaven on Earth. Praying, reaching up to God, connecting with our own God-Self, will help tremendously for all of humanity. We have the power to self-destruct planet Earth, and it appeared that we were on the road to doing that, unintentionally of course. Even though things do not seem to be too promising at this time, they will get better. We have to work through our own darkness and help the planet to work through the darkness we have shed upon it during our many incarnations. Now is the time for us to pull together and mend that which we have created from negativity. Allow the fear, hurt, anger, rage, bitterness, jealousy, etc. to be dissolved and replaced with Light and the positive energies of LOVE, Joy, Compassion and Forgiveness in your heart. When we reach this level, we will not only achieve inner peace, but Peace on Earth as well. Peace of mind will automatically result in a peace-ful heart and Soul.

What's going on is a wake-up call for all of humanity. It's not too late. There is still time! Find a way to overcome your fears. Instead of moaning and groaning, thinking that you cannot do anything about what is going on, pray! You do not have to say any specific prayer. Talk to God, the Angels, the Universe, and make a request for assistance from your heart and Soul. Expand the Light within you. Imagine that a beam of Light is coming into the top of your head from the higher dimensions. Bring the Light down into your entire body. Then expand your image of the Light encompassing all of humanity and the entire planet. You may not think this is real or possible, but your intention will increase the amount of Light that exists on Earth and will assist, not only in your personal Ascension, but that of Mother Earth as well.

I wish you many blessings during your journey on Earth!

Barbara M. Hardie

ABOUT THE AUTHOR

Barbara M. Hardie is the Founder and Director of Angel Connections, established in 1995 in Tolland, Massachusetts. Her mission is to help individuals open their awareness of who they are spiritually, to find inner strength and peace, to attract abundance, release negative energy which causes stress/problems, improve health and relationships, and to improve the quality of life in general through spiritual awareness.

She is an Ordained Spiritualist Minister, Certified Spiritual Healer, Medium and Counselor through The National Spiritual Alliance. She lectures on a variety of spiritual topics, channels the Ascended Masters and Archangels, and offers phone or email sessions designed to help individuals reach higher levels of vibration.

She is a Certified Master Hypnotherapist and received her certification through IACT — International Association of Counselors and Therapists. Barbara Hardie has combined her business experience, hypnotherapy skills and spiritual awareness in developing the programs offered by Angel Connections.

From October 1997 through January 2007 she organized/sponsored/promoted from one to five Mind-Body-Spirit Expos each year throughout New England and New York which she used as a venue to present information on *Creating Heaven on Earth— A Guide to*

Personal Ascension.

Barbara has lectured on spiritual topics and specifically the information contained in this book for the past 16 years to groups large and small throughout New England — in Massachusetts, Connecticut, Vermont, New Hampshire, Maine and Rhode Island; as well as in Albany, New York, Allentown, Pennsylvania, West Palm Beach, Florida, Chicago, Illinois and Bend, Oregon. During 2006, 2007 and 2009 she presented workshops and provided spiritual readings on the Royal Caribbean Cruise Line to destinations in the Caribbean, as well as Spain, Italy and France in Europe.

Visit www.angelconnections.com to learn more about Barbara. If you would like to schedule a private session or have a specific question, please email barbara@angelconnections.com.

Additional Offerings from Barbara M. Hardie

SPIRIT RELEASEMENT EBOOK

Spirit attachment is a very common occurrence and this eBook contains instructions to empower individuals to facilitate Spirit Releasement for themselves. *(Available Summer 2011. Visit www.angelconnections.com for the latest on this ebook and other offerings.)*

ANGEL READINGS

Allow the Angels and Spirit Guides to help you in knowing and understanding the situations that you are experiencing in your life. Feel free to ask questions about any or all areas of your life. *(60- or 30-minute phone or email sessions.)*

SOUL PURPOSE READINGS

Who are you? What are you supposed to be doing? Why are you here? Are you on your spiritual path? At this time many are restless, curious about what they are supposed to be doing. Let your spiritual guidance put you at ease in knowing what your purpose/life mission is for this lifetime. *(60- or 30-minute phone or email sessions.)*

The Angel Readings and Soul Purpose Readings can be combined into one session.

REMOTE SPIRIT RELEASEMENT SESSIONS

SPIRIT ATTACHMENT

If you think or feel that you have an entity or entities attached to your energy/auric field, Barbara Hardie can check to see if this is the case. If so, she can release them and have them escorted to the Light and then cleanse and groom your energy from any residue of negative energy the entity/entities may have left behind.

(This session can also be done from a distance and is usually done in the early morning hours.)

EARTHBOUND SPIRITS

If you know of an individual who has passed from physical form to spirit and they have not gone to the Light, Barbara Hardie can assist their Soul to their new home on the other side.

(This work can be done remotely through meditation and connecting with the deceased individual's Soul energy.)

RELEASEMENT FROM THE RESTING AREA

If a loved one has passed and you want to know where they are and if they arrived in the Light, Barbara Hardie can check on their whereabouts. If they are in the Resting Area (an area where the Soul goes when they are carrying a lot of negative energy), Barbara counsels your loved one until such time as they are ready to be received into the Light.

Visit www.angelconnections.com
Sign Up to Receive Special Alerts and Offers

Email barbara@angelconnections.com to:

- Order additional copies of *Creating Heaven on Earth* or to order the *Spirit Releasement ebook.*
- Schedule private sessions or request pricing.